Glass Bead
Inspirations

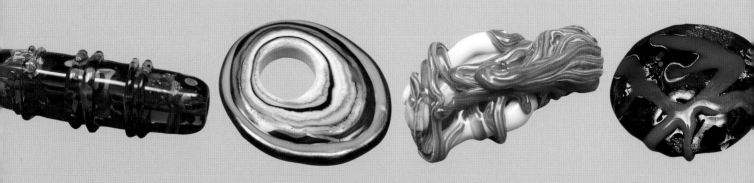

Glass Bead Inspirations

Ideas and Techniques for Lampworkers

LOUISE MEHAFFEY

Photographs by Kevin Brett

STACKPOLE BOOKS

To my very tolerant family
And to my glass tribe

> **WARNING:** Making glass beads is a dangerous process that requires using
> glass materials and hazardous gases and flames. Although safety precautions
> are noted throughout this book, they are not meant as substitutes for com-
> mon sense and caution. All persons who make the glass beads in this book do
> so at their own risk. The author and publisher disclaim any and all liability
> for injuries that may result from the execution of making beads in this book.

Printed in the United States of America

10 9 8 7 6 5 4 3 2 1

FIRST EDITION

Cover design by Wendy A. Reynolds.

Library of Congress Cataloging-in-Publication Data
Mehaffey, Louise.
    Glass bead inspirations : ideas and techniques for lampworkers /
Louise Mehaffey ; photographs by Kevin Brett. — 1st ed.
        p. cm.
      ISBN-13: 978-0-8117-0765-7 (pbk.)
      ISBN-10: 0-8117-0765-2 (pbk.)
      1. Lampwork. 2. Glass beads. I. Title.
TT298.M425   2012
748.2028—dc23
                                                                    2011020805

Contents

Acknowledgments

I want to give a special thanks to the bead makers who took this journey with me. (They are profiled on pages 116–119.) I am grateful that they were willing to tackle the challenges and then allow me to document their beads. Without them, this book would not have been possible.

Thanks also to the artists who permitted me to use their works to inspire the bead makers: Kevin Brett, W. Eugene Burkhart Jr., Adrienne Trafford, and three family members, Kelly Mehaffey, Denise Lecker, and Jeffrey Griffith.

All the photographs in this book are by Kevin Brett, who once again captured some wonderful action shots and documented all the beads.

I am also grateful to Kyle Weaver for encouraging me to write this book, and to the publishing company, Stackpole Books.

Introduction

Every artist at some time has trouble finding inspiration for new work. This book focuses on finding ideas for lampworked glass beads. It is not a how-to book, although I do include some techniques. It is my hope this book will point you in new directions to explore and that it may help new glass bead artists find their own style.

Lichen bead with metal leaf, enamels, and frit.

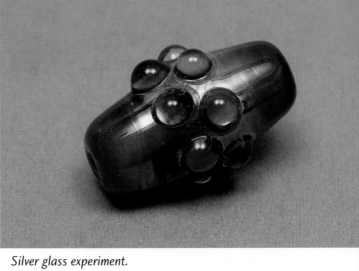

Silver glass experiment.

This book assumes that you know how to set up your studio and work safely, can consistently make basic bead shapes, and can properly anneal your beads. Beginners may want to refer to my book *Glass Beads: Tips, Tools, and Techniques for Learning the Craft* for the basics. The methodology in this book is to present a group of eight glass bead makers, including myself, with the same challenge and then document the resulting beads. When gathering participants for my book, I tried to choose bead makers with different styles and levels of expertise. Some of them are well known and some are not. Some have been lampworking for many years, and some are newer to the torch. (For more about the beadmakers, see page 115.) I wanted my book to explore some of the many different directions the same inspiration can suggest. Because there were eight bead makers, I hoped there would be eight different directions, and I was not disappointed. The resulting beads are very different, although you can see the connection. They clearly illustrate that one inspiration can have many different interpretations. Because some of the challenges are so different from the bead makers' normal styles, the designs are not all totally resolved, and that is fine. The beads represent different directions that they may choose to explore or not, and I hope the challenges have stretched their imagination. Their journey will hopefully inspire new directions for you, too.

The last section includes four step-by-step projects to demonstrate some special techniques, including making goldstone stringer, vine cane, and stamen cane; using pixie dust; blowing and using shards; and using metal leaf to create faux stone beads. To create your own vision of a glass bead, it helps to have mastered

a variety of techniques, so read, take classes, and most of all, experiment. I have shown how I do these techniques, but it is certainly not the only way, so don't be afraid to try something new.

At the back of the book is a resource list of more ideas that can be used as inspirations for beads. Use these suggestions as a springboard to new ideas and new beads.

In my own career of glass bead making, I have been very fortunate to have a group of friends who supported me, worked with me, and made me stretch my abilities. This is my glass tribe, which has developed over the years. In 1998, when I took my first lampworking workshop, I became friends with some of the other students. We kept in touch and took more workshops together. At each workshop, we made more friends, and our circle kept growing. Soon we started getting together every few months to work and share our discoveries. We came from many different backgrounds, which meant we each brought different skills and knowledge to the group.

After a workshop with Gil Reynolds, we set up Murphy fire buckets (small glory holes) to create pattern canes and other components, and began experimenting with making molds and casting glass. Today when we get together, we typically have a few people working on torches, a few people working with a fire bucket, and others casting glass. Someone coined the phrase "glass tribe," and it seemed appropriate. Everyone has always freely shared any information or techniques they learned, and as a result, we have all grown in our knowledge and skill level, and become very good friends along the way. I hope everyone is fortunate enough to have their own glass tribe.

Creativity

Creativity to me means being able to see new possibilities, new combinations, and new directions to explore. In other words, thinking outside the box. Creative people are willing to take chances and don't have a fear of failure. They are problem solvers. They have a great curiosity and because of this, they have a wide range of knowledge.

We can learn to be creative by practicing being creative. It becomes a habit.

When presented with a new challenge, think about it for a while and then forget it. Your subconscious will continue to work on the problem. Sometimes when you aren't thinking about it at all, a solution suddenly pops into your head. These *aha* moments are to be treasured.

There are many things that can help along the way. Think about your work environment and plan it carefully. Set up your work area in a way that pleases you. Have a comfortable chair in place, tools handy, kiln accessible, glass rods within reach, and good lighting available. For me, a variety of music, or sometimes a good audio book, is essential. I also have posters and photographs that inspire me on the walls.

Learn to recognize when you work best. Some of us are more creative when we are fresh in the morning, and others, like me, come alive in the evenings. Don't tackle difficult projects when you are tired.

Art is not created out of nothing, with no references. Follow your interests in many subjects and you will have a wealth of material to use for inspiration. Every project has parameters, imposed by ourselves, by an outside source, or by the medium itself. For instance, when we are working on a challenge, we can choose to focus on certain aspects ourselves, or an instructor can assign a project with certain requirements. Every medium has limitations. Glass has technical aspects that must be respected, and we need to recognize those boundaries to have success. But we also need to be sure that we are not limiting ourselves. Explore those boundaries and risk failure.

It can be a huge help to have people you can ask for an honest critique of your beads. Having friends or family who think all your beads are wonderful can be great for your ego, but not very helpful. Search out people who will give you their honest opinion, good or bad. You don't have to agree with them, but learn to seriously consider what they are telling you. Don't fall into the easy trap of just defending your work.

Set up a comfortable work area with easy access to your tools and materials.

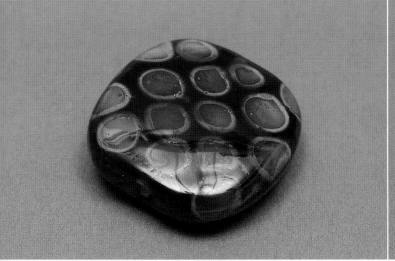

Silver glass dots, lightly reduced.

Wrapped tab made with metal leaf, enamels, and frit.

Also learn to critique your own work. It is very hard to be objective about your work because it is so personal, but it can be a very useful skill to develop. After every new bead, study it and decide if it accomplished what you wanted. Think about how to improve it or what new direction it suggests. By doing this, your beads will continue to develop in new ways.

Your Own Personal Style

When bead makers learn to express their creativity and create with their own vision, they will develop their own unique voice, or personal style. So what is your personal style and how do you know when you have found it?

Sometimes it is your way of using colors, making bead shapes, or decorating the bead, or it can be composed of many different elements. It is not static, and it continues to evolve as you create your beads. When people can identify beads as yours, you have found your own personal style.

It is always easier to copy something else than to develop your own style. When you spend most of your time taking classes and studying another lampworker's beads, it can be difficult to get beyond the teacher's style and find your own, but it is worth the effort. You can learn by looking at beads, analyzing how the beads were made, and what makes them attractive to you. Taking classes will expand your knowledge and skills.

Having a repertoire of techniques is very helpful when you are working toward your vision of a bead, but learn to use those techniques to express yourself. I love to take classes, and I try to find ones with in-structors whose styles are very different from mine. That way, I know I will learn something new. Experienced lampworkers know many techniques; their own style comes through how they use them. Once you have a basic knowledge of how to make beads, look beyond the bead world for inspiration.

People learn in different ways. Some artists depend on visual images, such as watching an instructor or studying a book or video. Some use their auditory senses, listening to instructions. Others learn kinesthetically, by touching and doing. Most visual artists learn primarily through their vision, but they can learn to use their other senses too. Listen to music and translate that into a bead, or feel a textured surface and let it inspire a bead.

Some people learn in a very logical order. In bead-making, that person will learn to make round beads well, go on to work on other shapes, and then work on decorating techniques, continuing through more and more difficult techniques. Other beadmakers will just jump in and make intricate beads, learning as they go. Regardless of how you learn and what your working style is, it is important to make time to just play and explore—try new colors, new shapes, and new techniques, sometimes working toward a specific vision and sometimes just letting the glass flow.

When I have a new idea for a bead, I think about it for a while and visualize how I want it to look. Then I think about how to get that look, sit down at my torch, and attempt to make it. The bead seldom looks like I visualized it, though. At this point, I analyze what worked and what didn't and try again. Even though I think about it beforehand, I usually haven't really planned on how I will make the bead. I seem to be

Artifact bead made using baking soda.

A foam bead made with metal foil.

more successful when I start with just an idea and let it develop as I am working. Most of my tools and a selection of glass rods are within reach. Because I am letting the bead develop as I make it, I never know exactly what I will need or where the bead will finally end up, but that is part of the excitement of working on something new. This style of working may not be for everyone. Some bead makers entirely plan their bead before they start melting glass. You should try both ways and learn what works best for you.

One of the hardest things about new work is recognizing that just because it isn't what you visualized, it isn't necessarily wrong or even a failed bead. If it conveys what you intended, then it is a successful bead, although sometimes the technique needs to be more refined. Sometimes it doesn't convey your intended idea, but that doesn't necessarily mean it isn't a good design. This is when being objective about your work is very helpful. Learn to recognize happy accidents and take advantage of them.

Punching through a Block

Almost every artist at some point will encounter a creative block. Bead artists will sit at the torch and wonder what to make. There are no new ideas, no new visions for a bead. Working constantly with no time for playing or learning can lead to a creative block, so no matter how busy your schedule, allow some time for recharging. Creating is hard work.

Here are ten simple ideas to help work through a creative block.

1. Spend torch time making simple beads. This process can be very meditative, and your mind can wander while you are melting glass.
2. Balance your checkbook, pay bills, or do some other mathematical activity. This is using a different part of your brain.
3. Do a chore you usually avoid, like cleaning the house. After spending time on a disliked chore, you will enjoy getting on the torch.
4. Read a good book or go to the movies.
5. Take a walk and enjoy nature. Better yet, take your digital camera along.
6. Take an art class that is not about glass or beads, such as drawing or painting.
7. Take a class that is not related to art, such as yoga, cooking, or bird watching.
8. Go shopping.
9. Take a nap.
10. Organize and clean your studio.

For me, the best way to create new work is to challenge myself to use something new as inspiration, just like the bead makers did for this book. Organize your own group of bead makers to work on challenges. You can take turns naming the challenge, or choose them yourself. Set a time limit, and then have a way to see all the resulting beads. If the bead makers are local, meet to see the beads; if they are not local, have them take photographs and email them to the group. Challenging yourself to work on a design you would not ordinarily tackle can open many new directions.

Happy torching!

Four Colors

Crawling

Italy

Entangled

Knots

The '60s

Fragility

Anger

Blue

Fall Foliage

Rock 'n' Roll

Abstract #3

Paisley

THE *Challenges*

In choosing the challenges, I tried to find a wide variety of subjects, including organic, mechanical, visual, emotional, and ethnic, and also ones that could have many different interpretations. Every two weeks, I sent out an email with a challenge to use as inspiration for a bead. Sometimes it was a photograph and sometimes just a word. I seldom offered any explanations or directions, and the bead makers were free to be very literal or not at all.

There were only two restrictions I placed on them: the glass had to have a COE of 104, and they had to make a bead (the definition of a bead is anything with a hole in it, so this is not very restrictive). None of the bead makers saw what anyone else was making, and they were asked to not discuss it with each other.

The bead makers were challenged the most by the nonvisual inspirations—not surprising because most artists are very visual. All the bead makers had favorites, which was usually something that related to a bead style they already made. The most difficult were the ones that were different from their usual style, but that is one of the purposes of challenges—to work outside your comfort zone. This is not an easy thing to do, but it can open new directions in your beadmaking. By exploring different directions, you will develop your own unique style.

Four Colors

I went to a home supply store, looked at their paint chips, and purposely did not choose glass colors. There were photos of rooms using a four-color scheme and I chose one of those schemes, being careful to make sure there was some contrast between the colors. The colors were ivory, green, brown, and turquoise. This seemed like a relatively easy challenge for the first one.

TAMARA: I made this bead several times with an aim to be exact about the color. It was hard to match exact colors with the glass, and the dark color was the biggest challenge for me. I am glad this was the only challenge of this kind.

LOUISE: Dots, dots, dots. I had been making a lot of beads with dots lately, so this seemed like a good way to experiment with the colors. The colors looked very different depending on the order I added them. I may continue to experiment with this color combination.

LAURA: I used the colors to make beads in my current style, so there was not much new. I liked the colors.

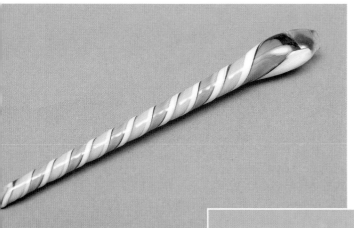

KATY: I love to create canes out of colors I don't normally use. It helps make them less intimidating for me to work with and expands my color palette.

PATTI: When I am experimenting with a new color scheme, I simply play with my standard designs and patterns. To combine a new color scheme, new shape, and new pattern creates too many variables and inevitably the beads are less successful. At first I didn't like this color combination, but after working with it, I changed my mind and will continue to explore its possibilities.

ALICE: The color chips looked like an unusual late-night television color test pattern. Glass color tests are a little different, but still require that different colors be lined up next to each other. I worked out a pattern that would lay each color against each other at least once. I loved seeing the reactions that can happen. I knew the ivory and nile green could be counted on for some fun results. To push along the test theme I added a sheet of silver leaf and foil.

NOLLY: My choice for the rosy brown devitrified (crystallized) to a dusty plum, but I stuck with it and the result is fairly true-to-the-inspiration palette.

CHRISTEL: The lightest color looked white on my monitor. Assuming the other three colors would be a little off also, I printed the four colors on ivory paper, hoping they would then be true. This is a design I have been making recently that uses only four colors. The turquoise-colored glass developed a metallic gray reduction film, so I tumbled it with grit in my rock tumbler to etch that off the surface.

Crawling

a Detail Photograph

This photograph by Kevin Brett was taken inside an old diesel-electric private train car that had been sitting empty for quite some time. The view is looking up from the floor to the ceiling along all the switches and controls. The image is precise, and I liked the movement and the mechanical nature of it.

LAURA: This was my favorite photo, but my least favorite bead. I remade this bead multiple times but was never happy with the result. I really wanted to capture the movement of the photo but felt like I just kept missing it.

LOUISE: As soon as I saw this photo, I knew exactly how I would make this bead. I used a Double Helix silver glass in the two-color twistie, but the edges blurred. Even though I was picturing sharp lines, I still liked it. Then I added the metallic dots to create some definition.

TAMARA: This one I also made several times. I wanted my edges to be crisper, and it's hard for me to do that in glass. In the bead I made, I was disappointed that the copper-green glass I used turned dark, and none of it can be seen in the bead. This was a loose translation of the idea.

KATY: When I saw this image, I instantly knew what I wanted to do. For this challenge, I enjoyed being as literal as I could in my own way.

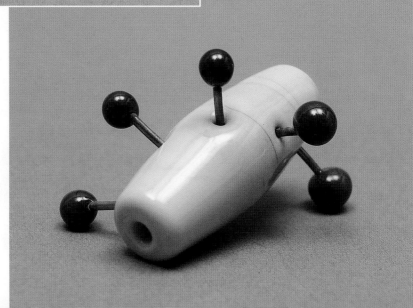

PATTI: The part that stood out for me in this image was the alliteration, and I tried several ways to emphasize that.

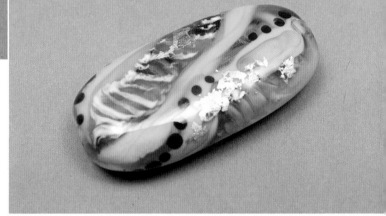

ALICE: This photograph was just the best! The color and curving pattern really popped for me. I worked on a twisted cane for the main pattern and tried to capture the wonderful shades of green.

CHRISTEL: I loved the colors and worked to match them. After making a twistie of intense black and white, I wrapped it around the bead and melted it in to distort it. Because the photograph was so textural, I added raised dots.

NOLLY: The swirling hammers definitely made me think twistie, with the round and straight parts speaking strongly to the work of German bead makers. I have never been very good at fine stringer work, but I gave it a try in this bead.

Italy

This country is home to some wonderful glass. There were many directions this challenge could take, and the artists didn't disappoint. This was the first challenge in which only a name was provided, no visual.

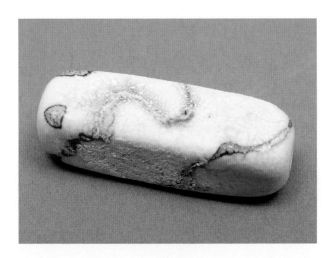

LOUISE: I kept thinking about the old walls in ancient buildings, sometimes with cracks in them. There is such a sense of history in Italy. I used baking soda to etch the glass a little to give it some age. (See page 93 for directions on using baking soda to create ancient beads.)

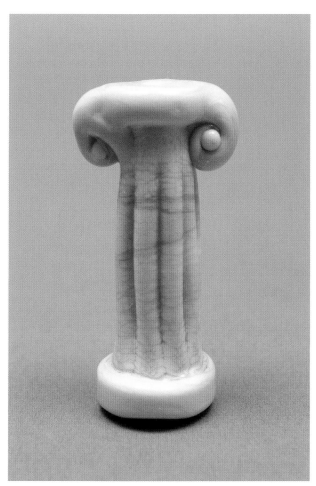

KATY: This was difficult for me because I had so many ideas for an Italian-inspired bead. When I think of Italy, I think of fashion, architecture, and fast cars. As a teenager I drooled over the Lamborghini, and I thought about a play on words—the lamb-borghini. I made a murrini cane (a pattern runs the length of the cane, which is then cut into slices to use) for the tires and then set off to make a fast sheep.

LAURA: Two things came to mind when I thought of Italy—food and ruins. I decided on ruins.

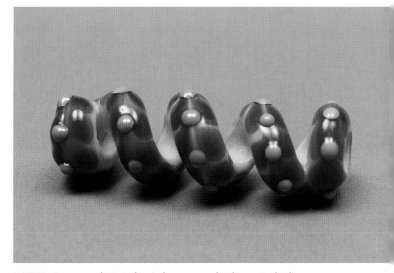

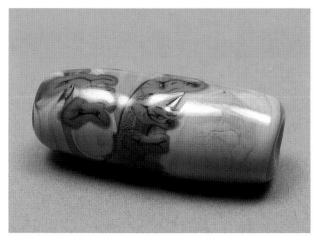

PATTI: I must admit I don't know much about Italy, but lately I have been enjoying twisty pasta, so that was my inspiration for the shape. I used colors that would bring out a Tuscan folk-art feeling.

TAMARA: I liked this challenge because I love Italy so much and have spent some time there. I wanted to capture the feeling of late summer afternoons with the warm sun, warm earth colors, and the contrast of the tall trees with the fields of grapes and olives that dot the Tuscan countryside. I think the bead has this feeling.

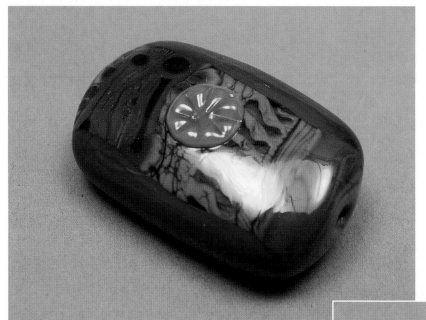

ALICE: There is an island near Venice where the homes are painted in the most amazing hues. I visited it on a cold wet spring morning, and while I was there, I came across a bright cherry-red umbrella. It had been set out to dry on a green wrought-iron balcony attached to an olive-green home. It was a sight I just had to stand still and drink in.

NOLLY: I have been making beads like this for some time. The color of the base bead is a Kugler 104 color, a true Tuscan deep ocher. The grapes were a natural, because I was preparing for a wine festival, so the challenge led into this series of beads.

CHRISTEL: My memory is blurry of my one day in Italy, but there were red roofs, white buildings, gorgeous blue lakes, green trees, and blue skies. For me, Italy is now about glass, beads, and millefiori (in Italian, "a thousand flowers"; traditionally, this is a murrini cane of a stylized flower). I am enamored with the challenge of building millefiori cane. This one has teal blue for the water, brownish red for the terracotta roofs, turquoise for the sky, and yellow for the sun.

Entangled
a Portrait

Painter Adrienne Trafford created this watercolor and ink portrait of a woman tangled in her own red hair. Very few of the bead makers make figurative beads, so I thought it would be interesting to see what they would focus on in this painting. Only half of them used a face or figure, and the others focused on her hair or the idea of entanglement.

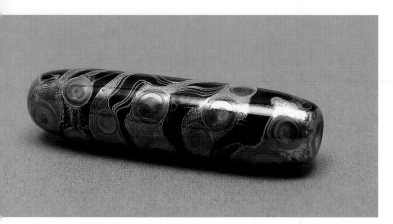

LOUISE: The way her hair wrapped around her body intrigued me, so that was what I focused on for my bead. I made a long, thin bead as her body and wrapped a lined cane around it. There was too much space between the wraps, so I added dots. I liked this bead and will continue to explore this technique.

TAMARA: I don't feel I have the skill to make the face or figure. I have the skill to make the feeling, so that's the direction I took—the feeling of being all tied up.

LAURA: I couldn't decide between doing a figure or a close-up of her eyes. I loved those colors. I was happy with the figure.

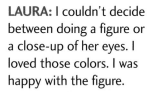

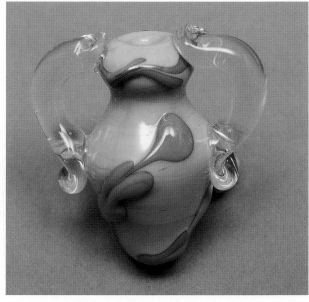

KATY: This was a real challenge for me. I didn't know what part of the painting to focus on. The hair spoke to me first, but I couldn't translate it into a bead I liked. Finally, I realized I could do the hair using the shape of a vessel to hint at the feminine qualities.

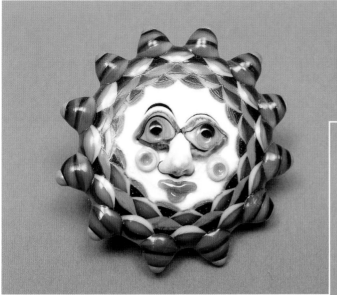

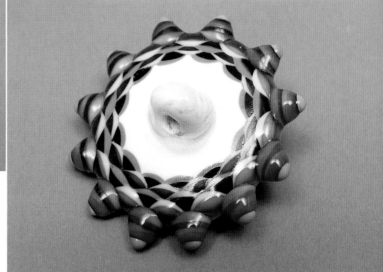

PATTI: I don't make much figurative work, but this project begged for a face. I stylized the hair's three colors to fit in with my own personal oeuvre. Also, I made it into a button, which is a bead, because it has a hole in it.

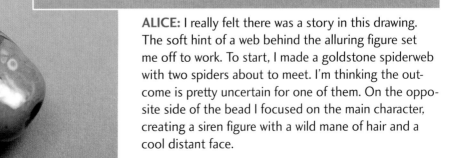

ALICE: I really felt there was a story in this drawing. The soft hint of a web behind the alluring figure set me off to work. To start, I made a goldstone spiderweb with two spiders about to meet. I'm thinking the outcome is pretty uncertain for one of them. On the opposite side of the bead I focused on the main character, creating a siren figure with a wild mane of hair and a cool distant face.

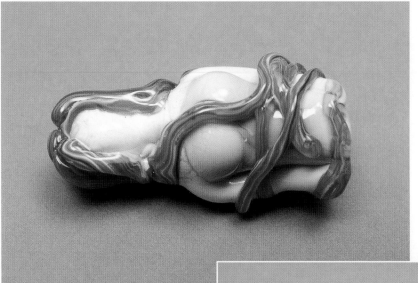

CHRISTEL: I enjoy sculptural work, so I chose to do this challenge as a sculpture. It was a bit of a dance keeping the whole bead hot while working on various parts of her, and I was very happy she didn't crack! The cane for her hair was made several years ago, and it seemed the perfect colors. I like viewing her from the back, with the way her hair wraps around her. She is "entangled."

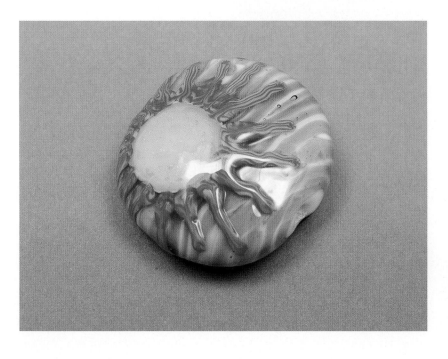

NOLLY: The bright ribbons of the woman's hair and the color of the background inspired this design. I mixed the purple by making an encased cane.

Knots

a Textural Photograph

This is a very organic and textural photograph by Kevin Brett. I thought it was interesting that almost everyone focused on the wood and knots, not the stones.

LOUISE: Textures really inspire me. I experimented with how to get all the lines in the wood using a lined cane, and then I rolled the entire bead in silver foil. It just seemed the right thing to do, and the silver created tiny balls, adding a pleasing texture. I think I will continue to make this bead.

TAMARA: I had a clear idea about how to make this one, using murrini as the knots, and yet I made a few beads before I was happy with the result. I found in all the beads that choosing the right shape was important. It seemed to be part of the language of getting the right feeling.

LAURA: I loved this photo and made multiple beads using opal yellow, ivory, and iris brown frit. I kept seeing a face in the grain, so that's what I made.

KATY: This was so much fun because I am drawn to natural types of beads. I enjoyed trying to replicate the cross-section look of tree rings in brown. Then I came back and added the knot holes and used a pick to pull the glass around it. I could have spent all day making this bead.

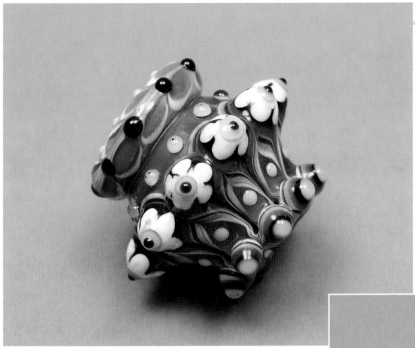

PATTI: What struck me for this challenge was the juxtaposition of textures and a beautiful asymmetry. By combining several techniques, I think the bead emphasizes these aspects. This is another idea I will explore more.

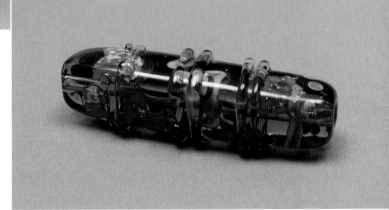

ALICE: All I could think about was fieldstone walls. I worked in neutral colors, created some fun shards, and added a few wraps of amber for a hint of warmth. My bead looks like an abstract stone fencepost to me.

CHRISTEL: I used stringers of different colors, passing around the dots that became the knots, to get the impression of wood grain. I was pleased with the spot where the ivory separated to give the impression of cracked wood around the knot. Tumbling in my rock tumbler etched the shine off and gave the bead a bit of old wood's soft texture.

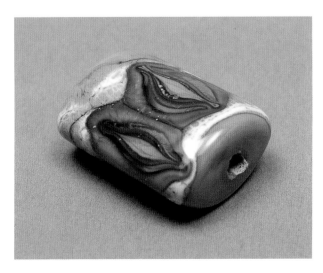

NOLLY: This was a real challenge for me. Should it be the grain of the wood or the shape of the stones? I ended up going for the layered look of the knots themselves, using silvered ivory stringer, and one or two of the silver glasses, and then raking the dots to simulate the shape of the knots.

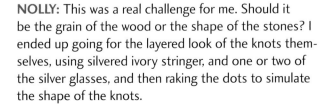

The '60s

Again, a nonvisual challenge. The colors for this one would be very different from the previous organic *Knots*. Not all the bead makers are old enough to remember the turbulent 1960s, but no one had trouble finding something memorable about that decade.

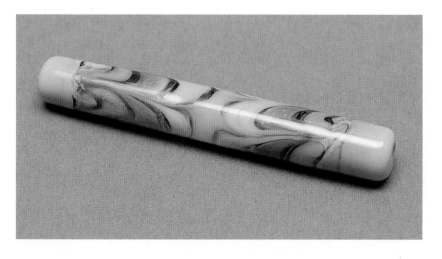

LOUISE: In the '60s, I loved tie-dyed clothing. In the '90s when it resurfaced, my kids and I tie-dyed T-shirts, which they thought was really cool. So for my bead, I used bright, hippy-dippy colors!

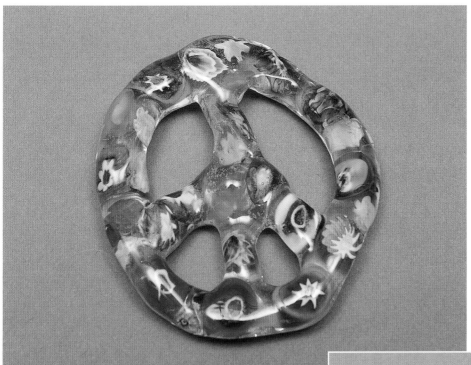

LAURA: My first thought was to do a flower, since the '60s flower is a theme I use in my work. I decided to challenge myself a little more and make an off-mandrel peace sign instead. I used some old murrini from my beginner kit to give it that flower power. Keeping the peace shape while adding the murrini was a challenge, and as I kept working, the shape became more distorted. I would have liked to tweak this bead a little more, but I was getting too stressed thinking about possible cracking and had to stop.

KATY: Of course "flower power" is all that I could think of for this challenge, and I wanted to use bright, almost neon colors. I created murrini with a flower Steinert mold and used all the bright colors I could find for the petals. I even used EDP (evil devitrifying purple, which is Effetre 254; it is called this because it can devitrify, or crystallize, in the flame). I made several designs with this murrini, some encased with clear, some with petals, but this version was the one I liked the most.

TAMARA: I tend to associate primary colors and geometric shapes with the '60s, something similar to the paintings I did then, although I find sharp edges difficult to achieve in glass.

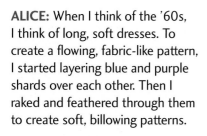

PATTI: There is nothing to say except "peace, love, and flower power, man!" We could use more flower power these days, eh?

ALICE: When I think of the '60s, I think of long, soft dresses. To create a flowing, fabric-like pattern, I started layering blue and purple shards over each other. Then I raked and feathered through them to create soft, billowing patterns.

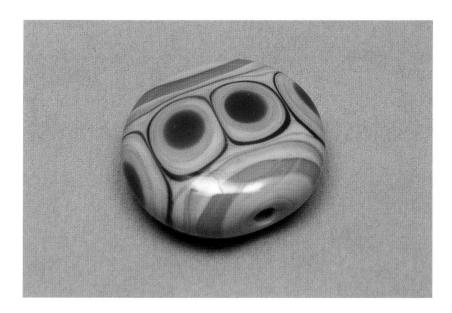

CHRISTEL: My parents had a clothes dryer from 1961 to sometime in the 1980s with pretty, pastel-colored buttons for the different cycles. I like pastel colors better than the colors that became "in" (harvest gold, avocado, brown, and orange). I had an idea in mind using the pastel colors, but the bead I made with the latter colors looked more psychedelic.

NOLLY: The peace symbol shouts the '60s to me. It was designed in 1958 by Gerald Holtom, a graduate of the Royal College of the Arts (coincidentally the same school attended by John Pasche, the designer of the Rolling Stones image; see page 43) to symbolize the nuclear disarmament movement. Since then, it has been absorbed into popular culture as a salute and call to action for everything from antiwar protests to simple human kindness.

Fragility

a Photograph of a Butterfly's Wing

The image in this photograph by Kevin Brett is striking, but difficult to translate into glass. The subtle texture on the wing is very interesting. Some of the bead makers focused more on the idea of fragility than on the image itself.

LOUISE: This bead took a lot of thought before I attempted it. I made a long, light, ivory cone shape to suggest fragility, and used a silver glass to get an iridescent sheen on one end. It took some experimenting to get the shade close to what I envisioned. I really like this bead and will continue to make it.

TAMARA: On this one I tried to go with the color suggestion. The puzzle always seemed to be how literally to take the challenge. The delicacy of the texture on the wing is difficult to do in glass. Always there is the contrast between what I can see with my mind's eye and what I can actually produce with the glass.

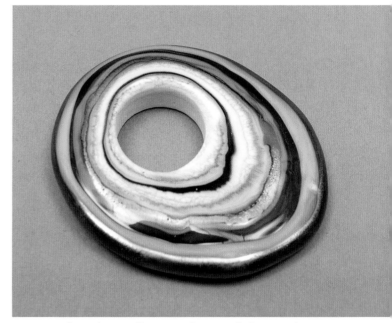

LAURA: The colors really inspired me, and I knew right away that I wanted to make this into a large-hole bead.

KATY: I struggled with this because I don't think of glass as fragile. It can cut and burn me if I'm not careful. I designed a pattern one might see on a butterfly wing and then used the lentil shape to again hint at the wing.

ALICE: This image made me want to see more of the wing. I created a fantasy butterfly so I could. I was thinking about two friends who passed away last year. The wings represent both strength and fragility, and the small figure is the determined soul that flies with them.

PATTI: I made this bead hollow to empathize with the idea of the fragility of the wing. I also created the design and used colors that were inspired by it.

NOLLY: I took this one literally, because I like sculptural forms, and it was a real challenge making a wing that could also be a usable bead.

CHRISTEL: Matching the colors and visual texture of the wing was done using Thompson enamels and then tumbling the bead. It is amusing to me that this bead is so solid, annealed, and seemingly indestructible, contrary to its inspiration.

Again, no visual was provided for this challenge, only the word. I chose this emotion thinking it could range from irritation to full rage.

LOUISE: Anger became rage, which suggested black and red to me. I didn't think far enough ahead to realize that I couldn't differentiate these colors when they were hot, so I just crossed my fingers and hoped the red would add to the design. (When red glass is hot, it becomes black.) I added little beady eyes, but I didn't want them to overpower the design, so I kept them tiny. My bead shapes are usually even and balanced, so I had to work hard to keep this one uneven.

LAURA: I was going to take this in a different direction, but after thinking about what I wanted to do, I realized I was carrying around a lot of anger. It was not raging and out of control, as I first thought of expressing, but a quiet burning deep inside. I encased the black and red core with clear to look like ice. I debated how much of the chill marks to leave, since I liked the texture they gave, but I am always careful to remove them from my beads, and habit is hard to break!

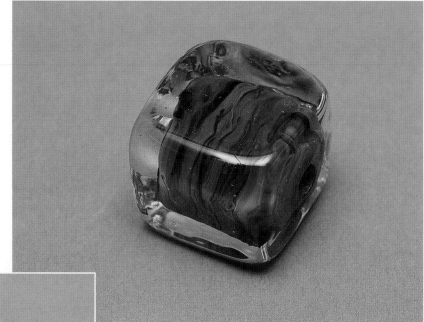

TAMARA: This one flowed really well, and I'm pleased with the result. I thought, yes, angry—black and red. And in glass it is so hard to see the difference between black and red when they are in the flame, so I added some silver to help it along. I think it did, but it still was like working in the dark.

KATY: I think of anger as being an emotion that swirls around inside you, infecting every cell like a virus. In this bead, I am portraying the swirling nature of anger in the structure of a microscopic virus. The pointy parts are how anger can explode in unexpected ways.

PATTI: Anger is not an emotion I feel when making beads, so this was a very abstract solution for me. I was thinking about what kind of bead I would want to throw at someone I was angry with. I would want it to hurt, so I made this bead like a martial arts throwing star, and I etched it to make it flat black with dangerous red tips.

NOLLY: What if you reached down to pick a beautiful flower, only to be bitten by a feisty daisy?

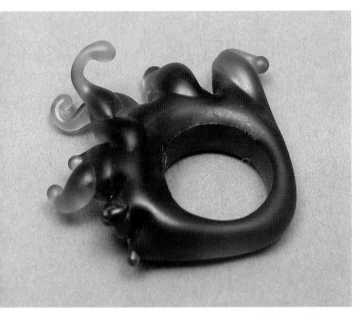

ALICE: To me anger seems to come in different forms and to be made of layers. I focused on passionate anger and created a sort of totem for it. The object I made can be worn as a ring or a pendant. The whole piece was etched to make the transparent colors glow slightly.

CHRISTEL: They say you see red when you are angry. I also see ugliness and chaos. Anger spreads too easily, like a disease. This bead looks like a diseased cell—nasty, pointy, and just plain ugly. I used scissors to snip and shape it, and I liked the reaction between the yellow and green, the ugly brown line where they touch.

Blue

The assignment was to use only blue glass or blue enamels. With using only one color, it can be challenging to have enough contrast, and sometimes texture becomes more important.

LOUISE: When I made a pile of all my shades of blue glass, I was very uninspired. So I added dark turquoise, a silver glass with a dark cobalt blue base, and teal. Now I liked the mix, and I left the last teal dots on the bead raised. They even fumed a little. I really like this color combination, and will continue to explore it.

LAURA: I played with layers of solid and transparent blues, something I often do, although usually not with only one color.

TAMARA: Just blue—a color I seldom use. So this in itself was a challenge, and it actually inspired me to make more blue beads. I made one beauty that had a lot of silver in it, but it cracked. Boo! This was the second bead I made.

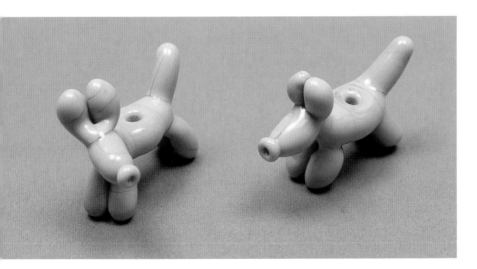

KATY: As I thought about this challenge I had several ideas I wanted to try. First I tried mono-chrome floral designs. Then it came to me: blue balloon dogs. I had been having fun learning how to twist balloons into fun shapes for my daughter, and I thought it would be fun to make a glass bal-loon dog. Blue is my daughter's favorite color, so this challenge evolved nicely.

PATTI: All color is relative. Where is the dividing line for blue and purple, or blue and green? I enjoy pushing the definition of a color. For example, when someone says blue, as in this assignment, I think of everything from turquoise through periwinkle, and I especially think orange! Color really pops when placed on its opposite color. So in the case of this bead I put purple-blue on yellow-orange, blue on orange, and green-blue on red-orange. There is a nice play on analogous color as well. It's fun to play with the very technical aspects of color.

CHRISTEL: First I made a large hollow blueberry bead with blue glass and Thompson enamels. I make life-size blueberry beads and incorporate them into my jewelry, so that was a little too easy. I wanted to play some more, so I dug through my odds and ends of blue stringers. Ultimately I chose this squashed barrel bead with the most shades of blue in it. I used heat, gravity, and a blue goldstone stringer as a pick to create the pattern.

ALICE: After I gathered my blue glass rods to make this bead, I pulled out some palladium leaf I hadn't used in a while. I am so glad I did. I had forgotten how much fun it is. I love the oil-slick peacock colors it can make.

NOLLY: Just blue? OMG, it is all about color for me, more than just one color! I haven't decided yet if I was successful using just blue.

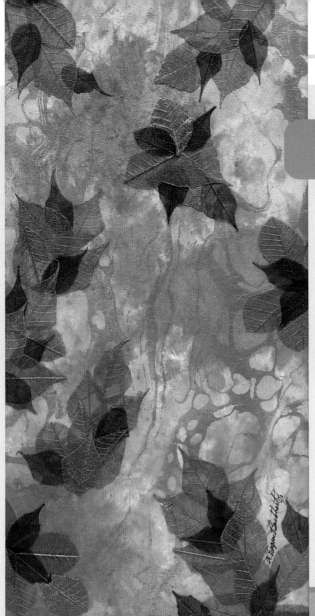

Fall Foliage

a Pressed Flower Design

The wonderful autumn colors and patterns in this artwork of pressed dried flowers by W. Eugene Burkhart Jr. lent themselves to many different interpretations.

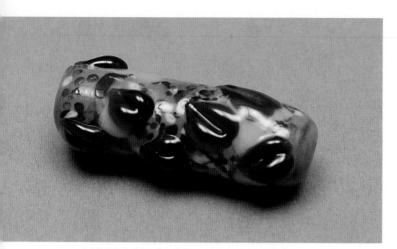

LOUISE: The background suggested frits, and I made my own mix to achieve the autumn colors I wanted. At first I planned to add two colors of leaves but realized the design was getting too complicated, so I only used one color for the leaves. I like the resulting color combination, but I don't like the bead.

TAMARA: Fall transparency. In doing this bead, I wished I knew more about making flowers. I didn't think I was interested in flowers, but I can see that there could be many techniques to apply to other beads. What my mind wanted to see was crisp, sharp edges with a transparency showing other crisp, sharp edges beneath. The result is not a match. It still has the feeling of fall with its color, just a little more rounded out.

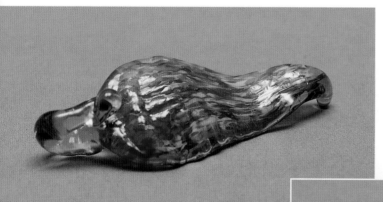

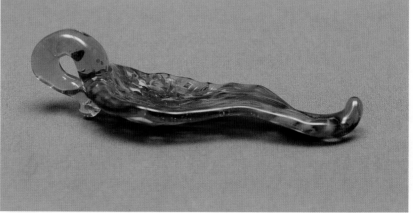

LAURA: Moretti and assorted frits—I didn't have to think too hard about this one. I liked the autumn colors.

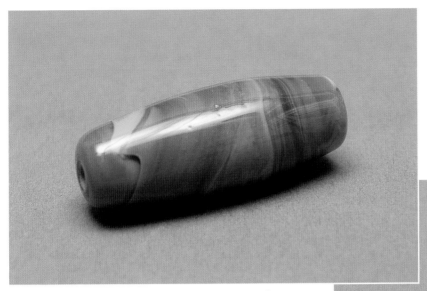

KATY: This artwork reminds me of autumn, my favorite season. What I love most about autumn are the subtle colors infused with a splash of bright color here and there.

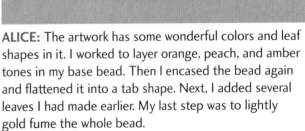

ALICE: The artwork has some wonderful colors and leaf shapes in it. I worked to layer orange, peach, and amber tones in my base bead. Then I encased the bead again and flattened it into a tab shape. Next, I added several leaves I had made earlier. My last step was to lightly gold fume the whole bead.

PATTI: I liked the soft, undulating colors and pattern in the artwork. I stylized it for the purposes of my bead, but I think it has a similar rhythm.

CHRISTEL: Fallen leaves by a pool of water are what I see in this inspiration. The shape of the bead is similar to a leaf, and I tried to recreate the colors, shapes, and textures of the artwork.

NOLLY: I considered this challenge for a long time before finally coming up with a bare tree, its leaves illuminating the ground against a dark fall sky.

Rock 'n' Roll

This nonvisual challenge is wide open to interpretation, and the focus of the beads varied greatly.

LOUISE: I thought about rock 'n' roll and some of its manifestations: Bill Haley and the Comets, Jerry Lee Lewis, the Beatles, Kiss, and heavy metal. Rock to me means a heavy bass, which led to large metal dots on my bead. The shape is tortured—shades of Janis Joplin.

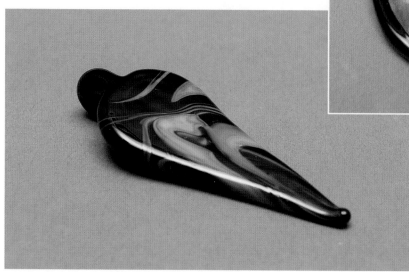

KATY: This was another inspiration that gave me many ideas to experiment with. I was thinking about how sound waves float through the air, and I wanted to show that in my bead. As I was thinking about rock 'n' roll, I felt that a musician is more likely to wear a funky pendant than a bead, and interestingly enough you can almost see a lead singer in the design.

LAURA: When I first received this challenge, I thought "yuck!" I spent a lot of time thinking about the anger bead and really didn't want to think about rock 'n' roll. I decided to take this literally—rocks and rolling things. The first thing that came to mind was wheel, and that seemed like a great challenge. I am very pleased with the first result and will expand on this design.

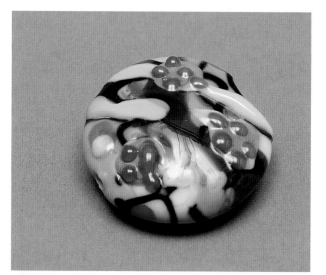

TAMARA: This one surprised me completely, because although I came of age as part of the rock 'n' roll generation, I do not have a visual to go with it. I love rock 'n' roll, but what does it look like? I was stumped, so I left this bead to make last, and finally decided to crank up the Rolling Stones and pick colors. I let myself freely make a bead, since it was my last one, and I had a really good time with it. These are not my usual color choices at all, but I like it. It's only rock 'n' roll!

PATTI: I have to confess I am a bit of a metalhead myself. My idea for this bead had to do with the cool shapes of electric guitars and the psychedelic colors and patterns found on album covers. What I liked best about the bead was that it also looks like a dangerous heart.

ALICE: This bead is hollow and super loose. I used silver plum (Effetre) to create fat shiny metallic lines that wrap all the way around the bead. I wanted to make a very fun and not too perfect bead. It is only rock 'n' roll, and I like it!

CHRISTEL: When I hear the word "rock," I think of granite, quartz, agate, etcetera. I have been interested in rocks since I was a child, and it was a fun challenge to make a bead that looks like agate. The Effetre Opalino glass does a wonderful separation, lace-like thing when juxtaposed with transparent colors. It mimics some of the internal textures of agate. The bead does roll!

NOLLY: This iconic image for the Rolling Stones was designed by John Pasche (www.johnpasche.com) around 1970 and has been used as the group's logo from then to this day. What is more rock 'n' roll than that?

Abstract #3

a Painting

Artists Kelly Mehaffey, Denise Lecker, and Jeffrey Griffith collaborated on this abstract painting. All the patterns and colors had many possible interpretations for beads.

TAMARA: This one was hard for me. I didn't like the bead I made much and yet I loved the colors here. I went back and forth about how important it was to get the idea of the longer shape in the bead. At first I was going to just go with the color and make a pretty bead using those colors. Then I decided the shape was important, so I went that way and could barely squeeze in any color because of the space constraints.

LAURA: This was my least favorite challenge. Neither the style nor the colors appealed to me. I was surprised that I enjoyed making the bead and was pleased with the result.

LOUISE: This was a tough one! I finally decided I didn't like all the colors, so I eliminated most of them and concentrated on the wavy line in the pattern. It seemed too plain, so I added raised dots. I was not happy with this bead.

KATY: I really wanted to replicate the design but struggled with tiny line work on a small bead, so I focused on colors and pattern while shaping the bead similar to the painting.

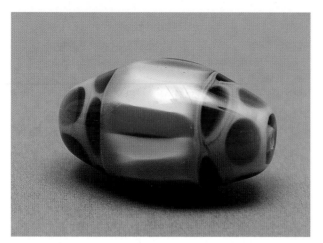

CHRISTEL: Here I tried to match the colors and some of the patterns. The barrel-shaped bead seemed to be a good vehicle for it.

PATTI: I have to admit I thought this was ugly on every level, but I liked the resulting bead. I used millefiori that I made and then twisted them. The overall technique has given me ideas for the future.

ALICE: This was a tough but fun bead to make. The colors were a stumbling block for me. I worked to make a bead that looked as if the pattern had been rolled up onto a glass bead. The top gray pattern turned out to be fun to make.

NOLLY: The color and geometric design spoke to me, along with the shape, which led me to make a bicone bead with raised silvered ivory stringer and a few pops of color.

I thought the rich patterns of a paisley print would be interesting in a bead. It is an old pattern, and if any of them didn't know it, they could easily find it on the Internet.

LOUISE: At first I was going to use tan, dark red, and olive green to make the pattern, and I toyed with the idea of doing it off-mandrel, but then I watched a home decorating show that used a cream-colored paisley wallpaper with a little luster and only one color. I liked the idea of using one color and playing with the texture to create the pattern, although I ended up using two colors. Reducing the bead really changed the colors of the glass, a nice surprise. I will continue to explore this idea.

LAURA: Really? I was hoping this last bead would have been a little easier, but at least it did not require a lot of thought. I decided to try an off-mandrel single paisley bead.

TAMARA: It's funny how people seem to have strong reactions to paisley; I find I quite like it. I associate it with wool shawls that come from Middle European countries and are used to drape over pianos and such. I picture them with lots of deep soft reds. This bead doesn't have those colors, but the way the shapes fit into one another satisfies a paisley "something," and although I would otherwise feel critical of the overall bead's shape, in this case it seems to be a paisley sort of shape.

ALICE: I have a very old, soft, washed-many-many-times, well-loved cotton bandana. It was my reference for the color and patterns of paisley.

KATY: Originally, I wanted to create a paisley design as in fabrics, with a variety of paisley sizes and dots, but it proved too complex. So I simplified and used two colors that created a tie-dyed look I loved. I added dots, melted them in, and then used a stringer to twist the paisley design.

PATTI: This was the most fun for me and my favorite challenge. I have been incubating the idea of paisley beads for several years, and perhaps this will impel me to develop this idea further. The smaller paisley bead (left) I made several years ago, and my skills are better now. I thought it might be encouraging to see both efforts, then and now, and see the improvement.

CHRISTEL: I love paisley! I had fun with this and made several beads but ultimately chose the first one. It captured the shape I wanted and the dots did some interesting things when melted in and yanked around into that paisley shape.

NOLLY: Paisley seemed to me to be a swirl of floating amoebas borne on a cloud of wispy threads. I thought that raked dots would be the way to make it, and then I was drawn to outline the amoebas with dots. That was probably overkill, but sometimes it is more about the process than the final product.

Projects
For Learning Special Techniques

Pixie Dust Flower Bead, page 52

To create your own vision of a glass bead, it helps to master a variety of techniques. Here are four step-by-step projects to demonstrate some useful techniques: making goldstone stringer, vine cane, and stamen cane; blowing and using shards; using baking soda to simulate an antique look; and using metal leaf to create faux stone beads.

Shard Bead, page 80

Ancient Bead, page 93

Warning: I am left-handed, so those of you who are right-handed will have to reverse the step-by-step photos.

Faux Turquoise Bead, page 99

Pixie Dust Flower Bead

To make this bead, you first need to make goldstone stringers, a multi-colored vine cane, and a stamen cane. Stringers are thin, spaghetti-like rods of glass. Canes are typically thicker and more complex than stringers, with more colors, although there are no hard and fast rules.

Techniques Demonstrated in This Project

- Making Goldstone Stringers
- Making Multicolored Vine Cane
- Making Stamen Cane
- Using Pixie Dust

Goldstone Stringer

Goldstone is copper particles suspended in a glass matrix. It is usually a sparkly gold color, but can also range toward a copper color. Goldstone rods, which are goldstone cased with clear glass, can be purchased, but when it is pulled into a stringer the sparkle is not very intense. By casing a chunk of goldstone with clear glass and then pulling stringers yourself, the sparkle is much more evident. If goldstone is overheated, the sparkle disappears. Even when cased, the sparkle can disappear, so be careful to work it cool.

Using Goldstone Chunks

A chunk of goldstone thermal shocks and cracks very easily, so it needs to be warmed before introducing it to the flame. You can do this by putting it on a steel plate on a hot plate, or by placing it in a kiln.

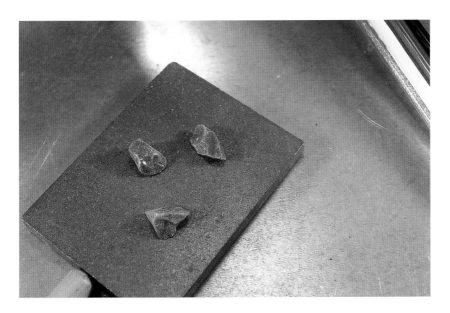

Here I used a large graphite paddle to preheat it in a kiln set at 950 degrees, being careful to keep the wooden handle away from the heat of the kiln. The larger the chunk, the more important it is to preheat it.

After fifteen or twenty minutes of preheating the chunk, heat the end of a clear rod of glass in the flame until the end forms a ball of molten glass.

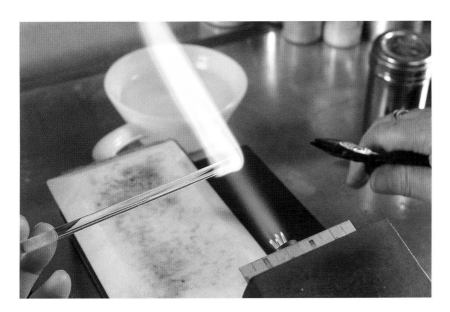

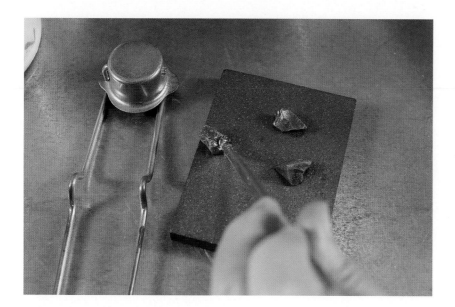

Pull the chunk out of the kiln and quickly press the molten ball onto the goldstone chunk to pick it up. If it doesn't attach, either the chunk or the glass rod is too cool. If this happens, return the chunk to the heat, reheat the glass rod, and try again.

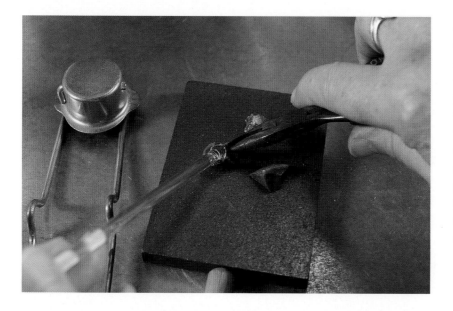

It can help to hold the chunk with tweezers while pushing the rod onto it. Once the clear rod is attached, move the chunk into the flame, heating it slowly to avoid thermal shock. Be sure to keep the section where the rod attaches to the goldstone chunk warm or it can crack and fall apart, but don't get it hot enough for the chunk to droop. Don't overheat the goldstone before casing it or the sparkle will disappear.

Heat another clear rod in the flame until there is a ball of molten glass on the end. This is the casing rod.

Place it on the goldstone chunk on the end away from the handle and push it toward the handle, keeping the ball of molten glass in front of the rod. When you reach the handle, burn the casing rod off. By pushing the clear casing on the chunk instead of laying or pulling it on, the casing stays thinner and air bubbles are avoided. Heat the casing rod again and push the molten glass onto the goldstone beside the casing you just applied, burn it off, and continue until the entire goldstone chunk is covered with clear glass. Heat the mass until it is glowing.

You can use squashers to make a more regular shape. Be careful to not heat the glass handle too much or the cased chunk will drop. If there are parts with thick, clear casing, you can heat and pull some of it off with tweezers to thin it a little.

There are two ways to pull the stringer. You can use a glass rod as another handle by heating the end to a molten ball and attaching it to the open end. Now heat the center to glowing and pull a stringer. Burn both ends off and set aside. Reheat and attach the two goldstone masses. Heat and pull more stringers, and continue until the goldstone has all been pulled.

Or instead of using two handles, you can heat the end away from the handle, grab a tiny bit of glass with tweezers and pull a stringer.

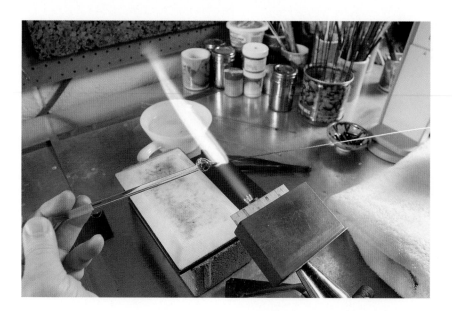

Burn the stringer off or use pliers to thermal shock it off.

Continue heating the end and pulling stringers until the entire chunk has been used. Make the stringers in different thicknesses so you have a variety to use. One about 1/8 inch thick is needed for the vine cane (or you can use a goldstone rod), and thinner ones about 1/16 inch are good for winding on a bead. Be careful not to pull them thinner than 1/16 inch or you won't be able to control laying them on a bead.

Using Goldstone Chips
A supplier once sent me chips of goldstone instead of chunks, and I discovered that they can make nice stringers too.

Heat up the end of a clear rod and push it into the chips to attach some to the rod.

Heat the chips on the rod.

Using squashers, press them into a rough cylindrical shape. Try not to heat the chips too much until they are pressed into the clear rod.

Now heat and pull stringers from this mass with tweezers.

Multicolored Vine Cane

To make a cane for the vines, choose four or five colors and decide which one will be the center color. In my vine cane, I used an opaque grass green for the center and added petroleum green, black, white, and a goldstone rod around it. If you want the black line to be more prominent in the vine, use intense black. Experiment with your choice of colors to find one that you like. This method will produce enough vine canes to use for many beads.

Heat about ³/₄ inch of your center color rod, keeping it cool enough so it doesn't droop. This rod will also be a handle.

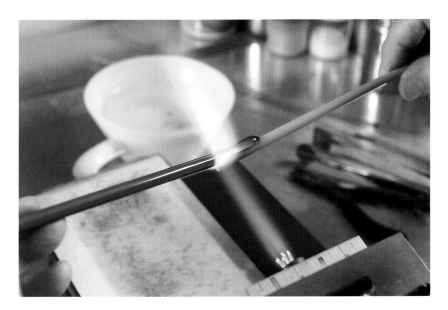

Heat the petroleum green rod and lay a line about ³/₄ inch long on the center color. Burn it off.

Heat the black rod and lay it next to and touching the petroleum green line, and burn it off.

Heat the white rod, lay it down touching the black, and then burn it off.

Heat and lay down the goldstone rod or stringer, and then burn it off.

The colors will be about halfway around the center rod.

Now repeat with the colors until the lines of glass are entirely around the center color. Adding more lines of any color will make it more prominent in the cane. Apply heat gradually from the ends to the handle to avoid trapped air bubbles. Heat the ends of the colors around the handle and press them down with a paddle or knife to be sure they are well attached.

To make another handle, choose a rod of glass. Heat the end to a molten ball and press it on the end of your vine, being sure to touch all of the colors. You can swirl it around to catch them all. Allow this handle to become firm.

Then burn off the center color on the other end.

Choose a rod to use as a handle for this end and do the same. Both handles need to touch every color, or when you heat and pull, you could just pull out the colors the handle is touching.

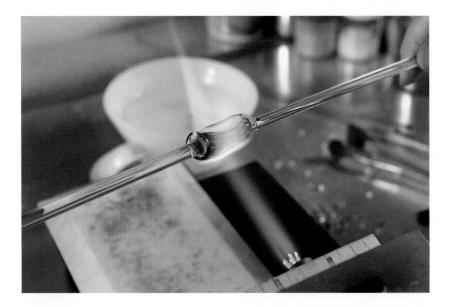

Now heat the center until it is a smooth football shape. If you feel like you are losing control, take it out of the flame to let it cool a little, and then continue heating it. This gives the heat time to reach the center of the glass mass.

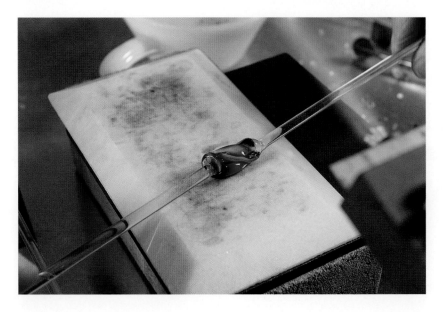

You can marver to help shape it.

Let it cool a little, heat a section, and pull your cane. I like to twist a little when pulling so the vine colors look more natural.

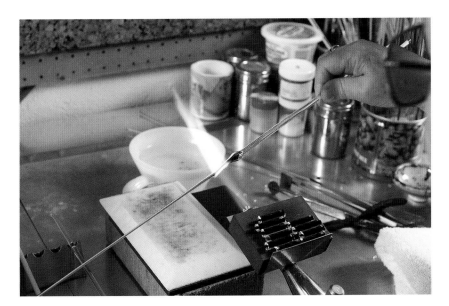

Burn it off and lay aside.

Heat both parts, rejoin them, and continue to heat and pull.

Or you can also use tweezers and continue to heat the glass and pull.

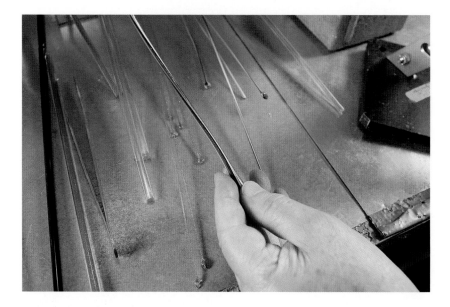

Pull them into different diameters, with some of them thick and some thin. Set aside a few canes to use in your flower bead. Clean off the ends of all the glass rods.

Stamen Cane

Filigrana is a rod of color cased with another color. In this case, I use a filigrana of black cased with clear, because I will make a white dot at the center of each flower and the black shows well against it. Plan your bead and decide what color of filigrana will work best.

Take a black filigrana rod and use a rod cutter or tile nipper to cut six or seven pieces about $5/8$ inch to $3/4$ inch long.

Set them on your torch marver to warm them up, or place on top of your kiln.

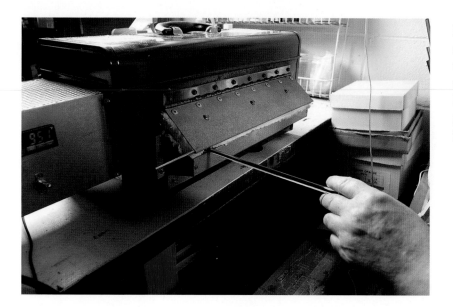

Heat about ³/₄ inch of the end of a filigrana rod; this will be the center of the cane. Filigrana thermal shocks easily. To help avoid this, heat very slowly in the flame, or place one end in your kiln for a few minutes to prewarm it.

Pick up a cut piece with your tweezers and warm it up in the flame, especially the side that will be touching the center rod. Be careful to not get the tweezers too hot or they will stick to the glass. If that happens, wait a few seconds and then wiggle the tweezers to loosen them. After the piece is attached to the rod, dip the tweezers in water to cool them.

Lay the cut piece on the end of the rod and heat to be sure it is attached, but don't get it hot enough for the rod to droop. If it does start to droop, straighten and cool it on your marver.

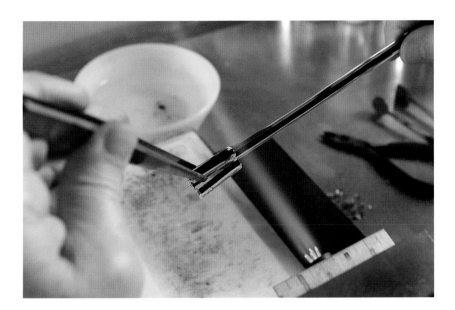

Keep heating and applying the cut pieces around the center rod.

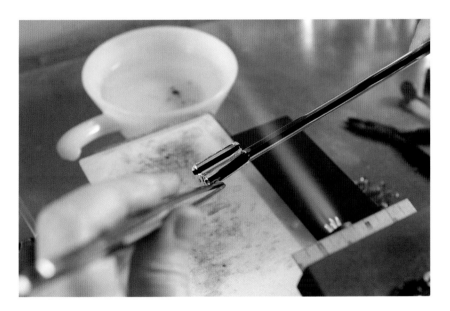

Use tweezers or a paddle to nudge down any ends not well attached.

Lay them so they touch the previous piece.

When the entire rod has been covered with the cut pieces, heat it slowly and carefully from the end to the handle to be sure everything is well attached, with no air bubbles. Heat the ends of the cut pieces on the handle and press them down with a paring knife or paddle to be sure they are attached.

Heat the end of a clear rod and push it onto the end of the filigrana, being sure to touch every cut piece.

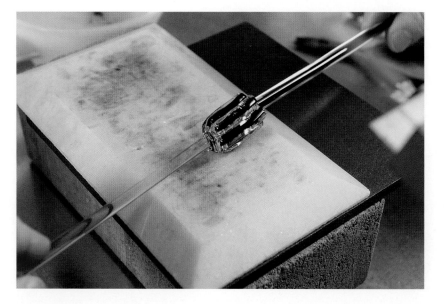

When this joint is cool enough to not droop, marver lightly.

Burn off the filigrana rod.

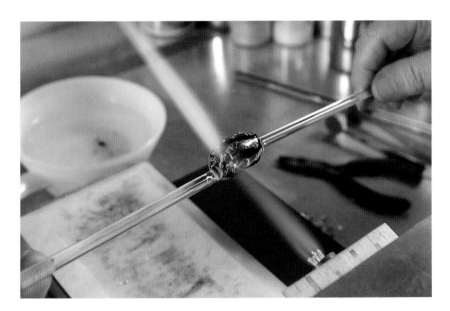

Heat a clear rod and push it on that end, touching every piece, so you now have a handle on both sides.

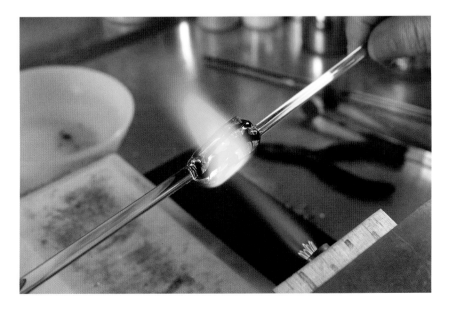

Now heat the entire mass of glass into a football shape. Marver if needed, and remove it from the flame; if you are losing control, to allow it to cool a little.

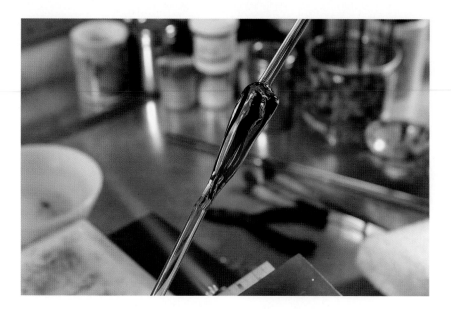

When it is a nice football shape, hold it out of the flame for a few seconds and slowly pull. Heat rises, so by holding the thicker end up, you can get a longer pull.

Burn off the ends of your stamen cane, heat and rejoin the filigrana ends, and continue pulling cane.

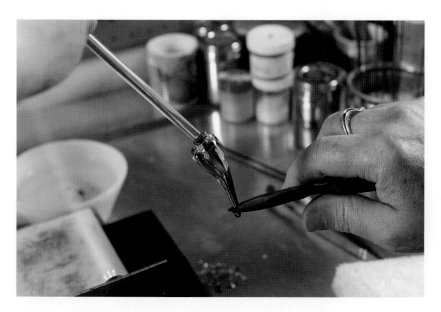

Or use tweezers, heat, and continue to pull cane. Pull straight, not twisting, and pull different diameter canes. Don't pull too thin or it will be very hard to use correctly. A good size is $1/16$ inch to $1/8$ inch. Set aside a stamen cane for your flower bead.

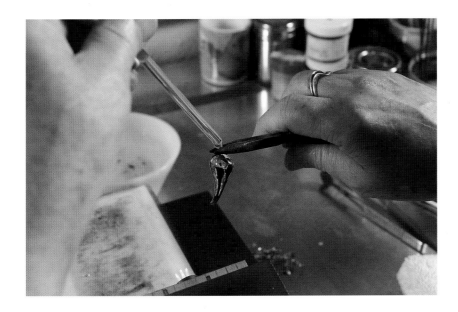

Don't forget to clean off the ends of all the rods by heating and pulling off the color, or cut them with rod or tile cutters.

Making the Bead

Pixie dust is powdered mica with an added colorant. Some of the colors are very dense and will cover any design under them. The colors labeled "hi-lite" are usually transparent enough to allow a design to show through, but test your pixie dust before using it on a large bead. As always, be sure to have good ventilation. Pixie dust has a way of migrating to your tools, workbench, glass rods, your hands, and anything else in your work space, so work carefully, and don't breathe heavily in its direction. When done, carefully clean off any tools you used.

Choose your glass colors. You need a base color for your bead, a petal color for the flowers, and a color of pixie dust. I am using a light transparent blue for the base, opaque white and dark transparent blue for the petals, and hi-lite blue pixie dust. A dot of white under the dark transparent blue allows the blue petals to stand out from the base color.

Transfer the pixie dust to a container large enough in which to roll the bead by carefully using a spoon. Form it into a mound.

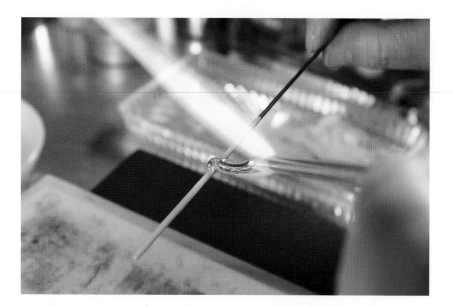

Using the base color, start winding the glass on the mandrel.

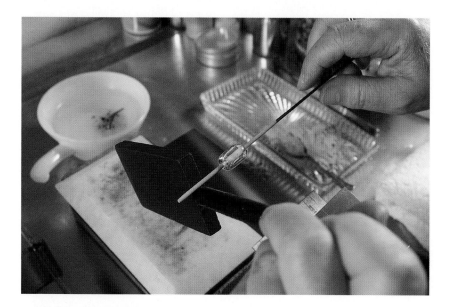

Use the crook of the paddle to rest the end of the mandrel while you are turning to check if the glass is centered.

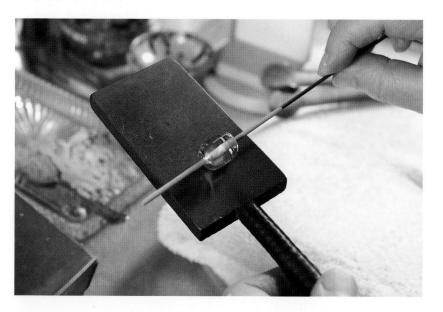

Make the bead a little smaller than you want the finished bead. You will be adding more glass for the vine and petals, so it will grow.

My bead will have four flowers. Using white glass, mark the center of each flower with a small dot. This will be a lentil-shaped bead with a pair of flowers on each side, so place a higher and lower dot on each side, leaving a larger space between the pairs. The larger spaces will be the edges of the bead.

Heat and attach the end of the vine cane to the bead.

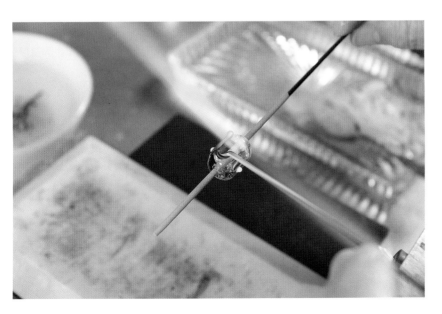

Wind the vine cane around the white dots and heat to make sure it is well attached. Melt almost smooth.

Add five white dots around the center dots for the petals. An uneven number is better than an even number. I like to use white stringers I purchased for this, but you can use a glass rod, or make your own white stringers.

Don't get the dots too close or they will merge when you melt them. Heat them to melt a little.

Add a dot of dark transparent blue on the white petal dots and melt them in.

Carefully heat the bead and marver it lightly to shape it. If you get the bead too hot or marver it too hard, the design will distort, so work carefully.

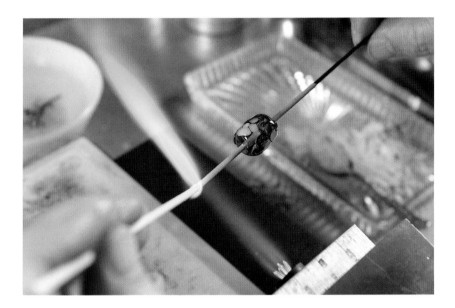

After much trial and error, I finally found a way to mark where I want to squash the bead. Heat the end of the mandrel and place a dot or wing of glass on it so it lines up with the larger space between the pairs of flowers.

I put wings on both sides of the mandrel. When I squash, I line up these wings with the edge of the squashers, which you will see later.

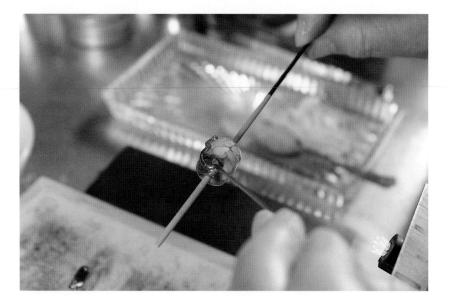

Heat the end of a goldstone stringer, attach it to the bead, and wind it around, burning it off when it reaches the first end. I usually follow the vine cane, crisscrossing over it back and forth.

Use a paddle to press and smooth the bead; this will speed up melting it smooth.

Heat just the center of a flower, put the end of the stamen cane in the center, and as soon as the white of the petals begins to turn opaque, rotate it, pulling the petals around.

A slight twist is enough. Snap off the stamen cane. If it bends and doesn't snap, it isn't cool enough. Blow on it to cool it a little, being careful to keep it away from your lips, and break it off.

You should see tiny black lines left behind. Do this for all four flowers. The more you twist, the longer the black lines.

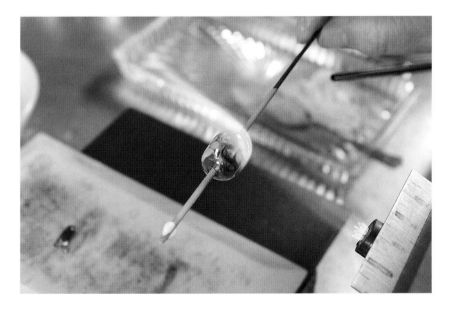

Twisting the petals with the cane will leave indentations, which you can leave, or gently heat to smooth them out. Turn the bead so your light shines on the flower centers to be sure they are smooth. Now heat and marver to get a balanced shape.

Before squashing, check to be sure your wings are still correct. If not, add two more.

Heat, line up the wings on the edge of the squashers, and squash. I am using Oneida ice tongs to get a gentle lentil shape. Use any squasher or bead press to get the shape you want.

Flip and squash.

Check the shape and gently make any corrections with a graphite paddle. Flame-polish the chill marks, and heat the bead to a dull glowing red.

Roll it in the mounded pixie dust, being careful to not touch the container with the bead, because the glass is hot enough to become deformed. I like to roll it at least twice, being sure to cover the sides and ends of the bead. Work quickly so the bead doesn't cool too much.

Now gently heat the bead in the flame, turning it quickly. The pixie dust will scum if it gets too much heat, so be careful.

Place in the kiln for annealing.

Shard Bead

This bead has a light sifting of a Thompson enamel (COE 104), 28-gauge fine silver wire (fine silver is 100 percent silver; sterling silver won't work because there is copper in it), and shards with silver foil, and finally I reduced it. Making your own shards of glass and adding them to a bead can open up many design possibilities.

Technique Demonstrated in This Project

• Blowing and Using Shards

The shards are made by blowing a bubble of glass and breaking it into pieces, or shards. Any color can be used, although some colors will be easier to blow than others. The softer colors, like white and ivory, are the hardest to blow. I am using an Effetre dark teal glass. With silver foil, it has a wonderful reaction in a reduction flame. You can also wind twisties or canes on the bubble, decorate it with dots, or use just about any other decorative technique. Just remember that the glass will become much thinner when it is blown into a bubble, so colors will be much lighter. If you are combining colors, be sure to use strong contrasting ones.

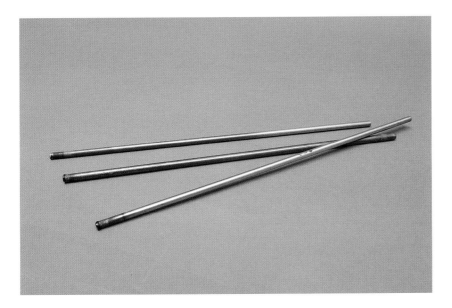

There are small blowpipes just like the larger ones that glass blowers use, but a stainless steel tube about 12 inches long will work just as well. The diameter doesn't matter too much, although it probably shouldn't be larger than $1/4$ inch. The smaller the diameter, the smaller the hole on the glass bubble, and therefore the more usable glass on the bubble. The tubes can be purchased from any lampwork supplier. I am using a tube with an ID (inner diameter) of $1/8$ inch and a length of 12 inches, because that is what I had.

Shards

Start by heating the end of the tube and then winding the glass on the bare metal on the end of the tube. This is just like making a hollow bead. **Warnings:** Do not use bead release. Do not plug the tube with glass. Do not put the tube in water. If the inside is wet, it will create steam when it is heated, which is hot.

Continue winding the glass into a spiral, building it straight up from the tube.

Then wind it out, and then wind it closer and closer to close the bubble. Try to keep the thickness of the glass even.

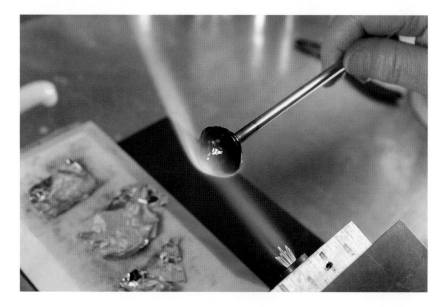

When the bubble is closed, heat it and turn the tube to keep it centered.

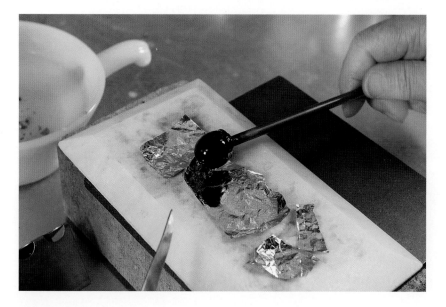

Now decorate it however you choose. I am rolling it in silver foil, covering it completely.

Burnish the foil with a paring knife or tweezers. In this case, foil is better than leaf, because it is thicker. Remember it will become thinner when the bubble is blown.

Burn the silver into the glass.

Heat the bubble. It is very important that you turn the tube at an even rate to heat the bubble evenly.

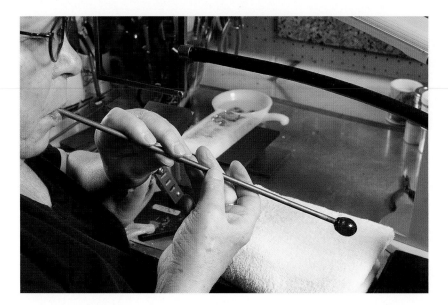

As you are turning, quickly move the tube to your mouth and puff gently into it several times to help center and cool it. Puff quickly, less than one second in duration, and continue to turn the tube. Don't blow yet. By holding the tube downward a little, you can watch what is happening to the glass. Keep it centered.

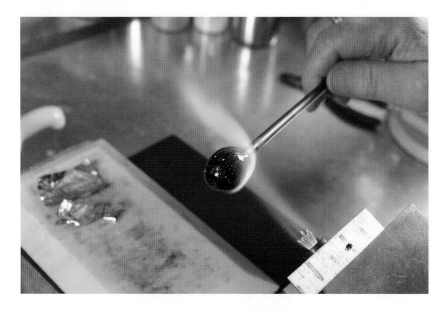

Move the bubble back to the flame and heat again. Heating and puffing several times will help get the glass to an even thickness and center it. You are expanding and contracting the bubble a little each time you do this.

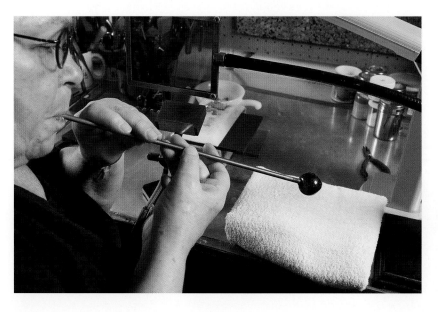

When you feel that it is centered, evenly heat the bubble. Then move the tube to your mouth while continuing to turn and blow. Start by puffing or blowing gently and watch the bubble. Keep it centered by turning. If the bubble is not getting larger, puff or blow a little harder. If it isn't enlarging, return it to the flame, heat, and try again. I like to get the bubble started by puffing, and once it begins to enlarge, I then blow gently. Don't blow too hard or you will blow a hole in the bubble; that can release tiny pieces of glass into the air that you can accidently inhale, which can be dangerous. Be sure you have good ventilation. As you blow, watch for thin spots that may develop, and if that happens, stop blowing.

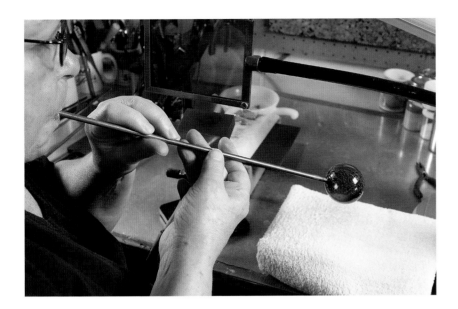

I like to blow round bubbles for the practice, but because we are breaking the bubble into shards, it really doesn't matter if it is uneven.

Place the tube with the bubble on the end in a clean metal container, such as a coffee can. In five minutes or so, you may hear a crack as the glass and tube cools and contracts at different rates. Sometimes the glass bubble will pop off the tube on its own. If it doesn't, just hit the tube sharply with something like metal pliers to shock it off.

Use something heavy, like pliers or large screwdriver, to break the bubble. I am using a heavy large mandrel. Cover the can first, so that little bits of glass don't float into the air, and hit the bubble to break it.

When the pieces are broken into the sizes I want, I gently move the shards into a canister for storage. Be careful that small pieces don't float into the air. Each canister is marked with the color of glass and decorative technique.

Pick through the shards and lay some on your marver, so they are ready to use. I'll also use some enamel, so I have that ready on a saucer with a little sifter.

Cut a length of fine silver wire. I'm using the flame to cut it. This is 28-gauge wire, but 26- or 30-gauge will work fine. (The smaller the number, the thicker the wire.) The silver wire will form balls when the flame hits it, and if the wire is too thick, these balls can be too large to stay on the bead.

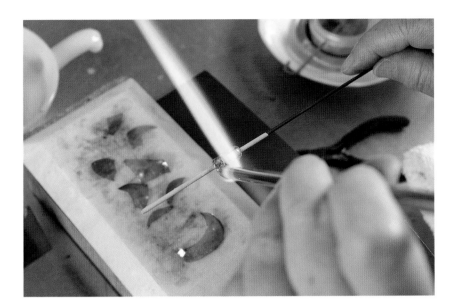

Making the Bead

Make a base bead.

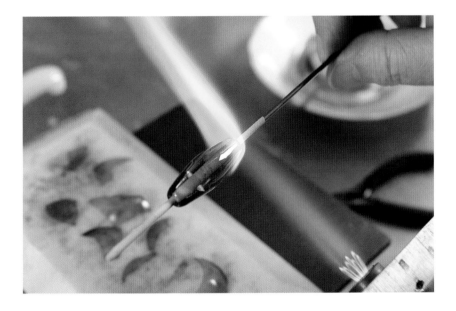

Complete the bead to the desired shape and size.

Sift a little enamel on the bead.

Heat the enamel to make sure it is well attached. You can leave it a little rough or melt it smooth.

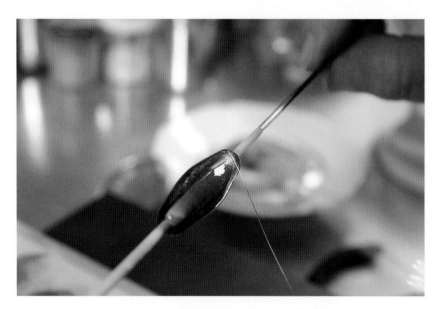

Lay one end of the wire on an end of the bead and slowly move it toward the flame until it melts enough to stick to the glass. Move very slowly—the wire is so thin it will melt very quickly. Also, the wire transmits heat, so keep your fingers back.

When the end is stuck, turn the bead so the wire winds around it.

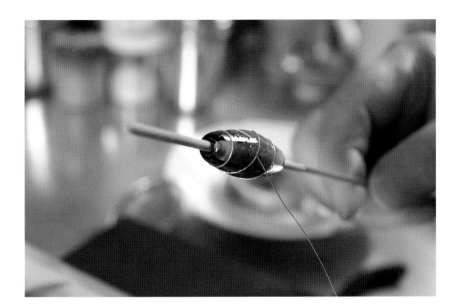

Wind to the other end of the bead, and then wind back.

When the wire is back to the first end, burn it off. Heat the wire on the entire bead; it will form little balls of silver.

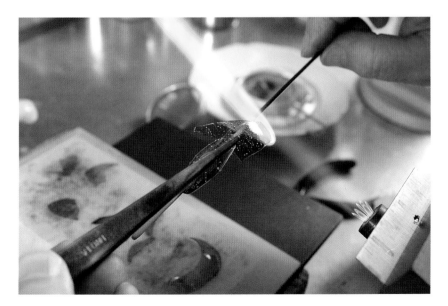

Pick up a shard with tweezers and warm one end of it in the flame.

Apply that end to the bead.

Gently warm the shard, starting from the end that is attached, and as it softens, press it onto the bead with tweezers or a paddle.

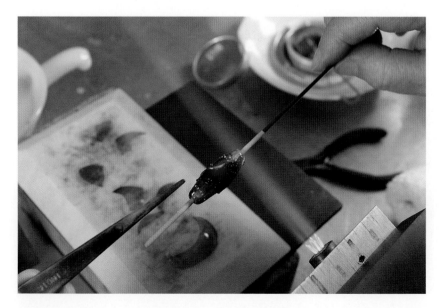

Check to be sure that all edges of the shard are attached. Heat and press them with a paddle or tweezers. Don't heat too much or the edges will start to round up, unless that is what you want. For this bead, I want the shards to be distinct, not melted into the bead.

Continue to add shards until a pleasing design is achieved. Remember to warm the entire bead occasionally, and keep both ends warm. Cool the tweezers in water if they get too hot.

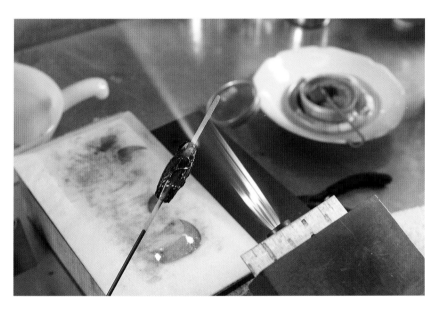

Change the torch to a reduction flame (an oxygen-starved flame) by either turning the propane up or turning the oxygen down. A light reduction flame will be a little yellow, and a heavy reduction flame will be very yellow. Different glass and metals react differently, so experiment. Start with a light reduction flame, and if that doesn't create a reaction, increase the propane. There is a mystery to reduction. Some days it works very well and other days it won't work at all. Many factors can influence it—the chemistry of the flame, the color of the glass, the temperature of the glass and flame, and some other factors I haven't discovered yet, so keep experimenting.

To reduce, allow the bead to cool a little. Now move it in and out of the reduction flame as you turn the bead. One second in the reduction flame is all that is needed. Put it in the flame for one second, take it out, turn it and put it back in the flame, take it out, turn, and continue. If no reduction is happening, try putting the bead into the flame closer to the torch, further out in the flame, or increase the gas in the flame. Reduction happens almost immediately, so if none of this causes that metallic sheen, it probably isn't going to happen. While doing all this, be sure to keep the bead warm.

Place in the kiln for annealing.

Ancient Bead

By rolling a bead in baking soda, it can look like it was buried for hundreds of years. Some glass colors will react more than others, so don't be afraid to experiment.

Technique Demonstrated in This Project

• Using Baking Soda to Simulate Aging

To prepare, spoon some baking soda into a metal ashtray or saucer. I like to use a metal ashtray, because I can bend it into a U shape to roll a bead in it. This is especially handy for frits (crushed glass).

First make a base bead. I am using light ivory.

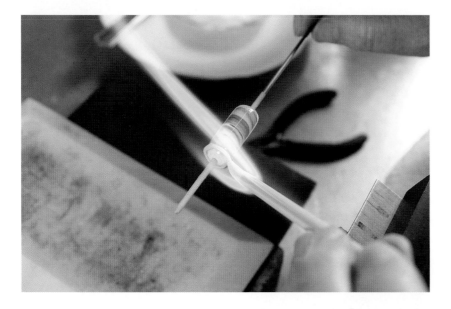

I plan to use my squashers to make a long rectangular bead, so I want it about 2 inches long and about $^1/_2$ inch thick.

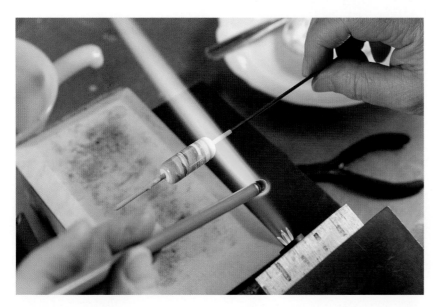

I want to wind a turquoise stringer on the bead, and I forgot to make it before I started the bead, so I am making an emergency stringer. While keeping my bead warm, I heat the end of the turquoise glass rod.

Quickly warm the end of the mandrel, touch the turquoise rod to it, and pull a stringer.

When the glass hardens, the stringer sometimes pulls off the mandrel. If it doesn't, burn it off the mandrel, and then burn it off the rod. Because there isn't much glass in the stringer, it will cool enough to use very quickly. Keep your bead warm.

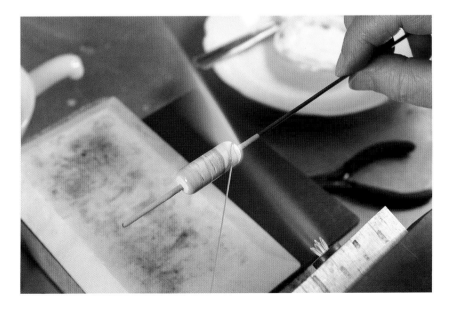

Heat the end of the stringer to attach it to the bead.

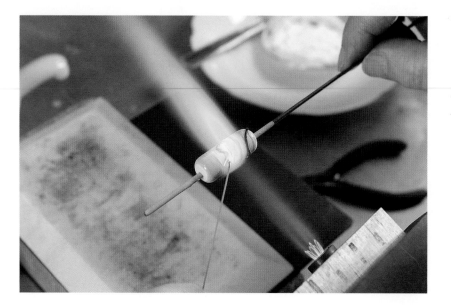

Keep the stringer on the side of the flame so it doesn't get too hot. Wind it onto the bead. By working on the side of the flame, it is easy to move closer to the flame or away from it to control the heat. Think of "writing" with the stringer as moving the bead, not the stringer.

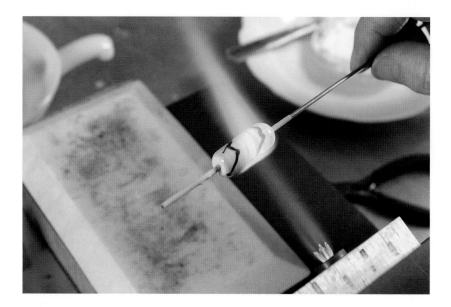

Heat the bead to melt the stringer into it.

Roll the bead in the baking soda. If that doesn't cover the bead, touch the bead to the baking soda, turn and touch again, and continue until the bead is covered.

Return it to the flame and heat.

Roll or touch it to the baking soda again. You can also use a spoon to hold the baking soda.

Return it to the flame. Continue to heat and touch to the baking soda until you have the effect you want. The more times you do this, the more "etching" will occur. I rolled this bead in baking soda five or six times for a strong etch.

Heat the bead to an even temperature. Using the squashers, press quickly but gently. Because the squashers are not truly parallel, turn the bead over and press again. Don't press too much or you will not be able to form a rectangular shape.

Turn the bead a quarter-turn and gently press; then turn it over and press again. It helps to press at eye level and watch the end of the bead to make sure it is a rectangular shape. If the bead cools too much to squash, heat it in the flame and continue squashing until you get the shape you want. Remember to flame-polish chill marks.

When you are satisfied with the results, put the bead in your kiln for annealing, not touching any other beads. After the bead is annealed and removed from the mandrel, be sure to wash it well. Rinsing it in vinegar will counteract any remaining baking soda. An old toothbrush is good for scrubbing. Be sure to clean it well because any remaining baking soda will continue to react with the glass and with any glass it touches.

Faux Turquoise Bead

The bead below is before etching, and it is a good example of recognizing happy accidents and taking advantage of them. The first time I made this bead I thought it was truly ugly. With nothing to lose at that point, I tried etching it (left), and discovered it now looked like turquoise. When I string it with turquoise stones, it looks like a natural stone.

Technique Demonstrated in This Project

• Using Metal Leaf and Etching to Simulate Stone

To make this bead, I will be using silver and copper leaf and intense black stringers, and when cool, it will be etched. I like to keep some silver and copper leaf in a shallow box, especially the pieces I tore from a full sheet. Keeping them in a box helps to keep the air currents from moving them.

Start by picking out or making silver leaf strips and placing them on your marver. I like to tear the strips to get an irregular edge rather then cut them. (If your hands are dry, you can carefully tear the leaf. If your hands are moist at all, the leaf will stick to them; layer the leaf between sheets of paper and tear or cut them.) After using the silver leaf, we will be rolling the entire bead in copper leaf, so have a piece large enough for that, plus some extra pieces for patches.

Pull some thin intense black stringers. Intense black will remain black even when pulled thin. It has some metal in it and is more expensive than regular black, so I usually buy it in a stringer form that is 2 or 3 mm thick. Heat one end to a ball and use pliers or tweezers to pull a stringer. It should be thinner than you usually make stringers, but not as thin as a strand of hair.

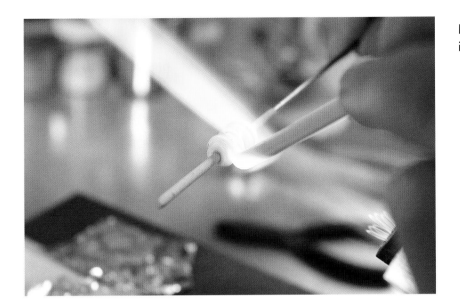

Make a base bead. I am using light ivory.

If the glass is not centered, heat it until it begins to form a ball in the center of the bead. Center the ball by putting the end of the mandrel in the crook of the paddle and turn, pausing just slightly when the larger part is at the top.

Keep turning and wait for the glass to cool a little. Roll it gently on the paddle. If it is still not centered after doing this several times, the mandrel may be bent. When starting a large bead, first check the mandrel to be sure it is straight.

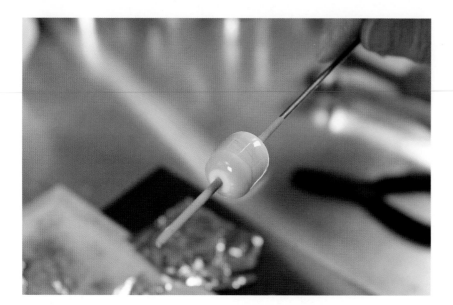

I plan to squash the bead with my ice tongs, so it needs to be about ⅝ inch long and ½ inch thick.

Heat the bead and roll it on a strip of silver leaf.

Use tweezers or a paring knife to burnish, or rub, it smooth. If the leaf doesn't stick to the glass, then the glass wasn't hot enough. Heat it and try again.

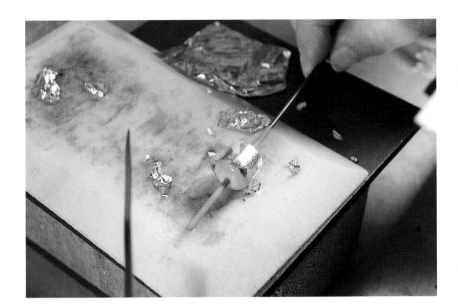

Roll it on another strip of silver leaf. Have the strips somewhat evenly spaced around the bead, but don't cover the entire bead. Be sure to burnish each strip as you add it.

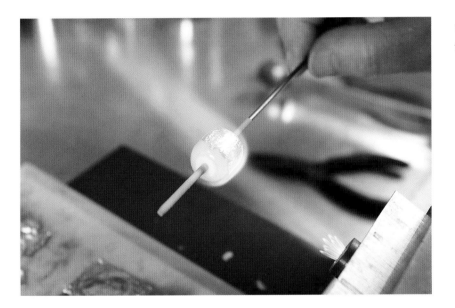

When done adding silver leaf, heat the bead well.

Now roll the bead on a large piece of copper leaf. I like to have the bead a little cooler for this, because if the glass is really hot, the copper leaf will "flash" and oxidize very quickly, which makes it difficult to manage. You can see some oxidation on the copper leaf where it is touching the bead.

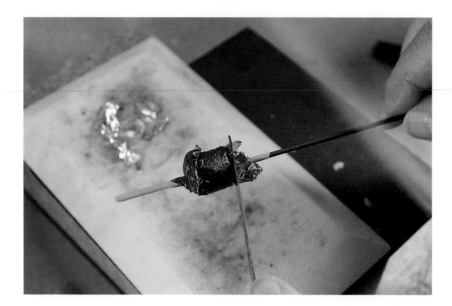

Gently push the ends of the copper foil in around the mandrel.

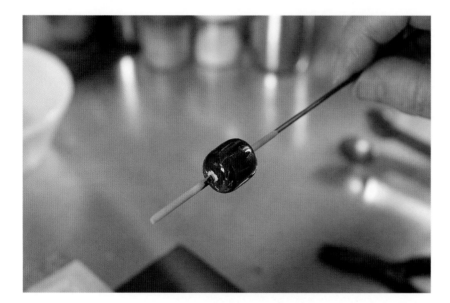

Heat the bead.

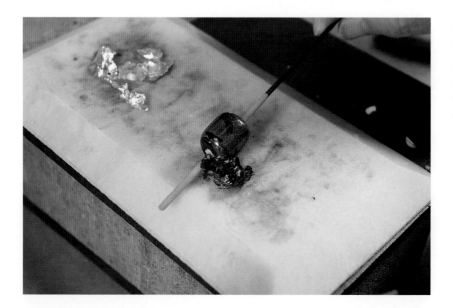

If you see any holes in the copper leaf, patch them with small pieces of copper leaf. Continue with this until the entire bead is covered with copper leaf. Heat the bead well.

Heat the end of the thin, intense black stringer and attach it to one end of the bead. As it is heated, it will form a ball, which you don't want, so don't work too hot.

Working below the flame, wind it around the bead toward the other end and then back again. I like to work below the flame, because it is very easy to move up or down a little to control the heat. Because the stringer is so thin, it will melt very easily, so work slowly and a little cool.

Flame cut the stringer.

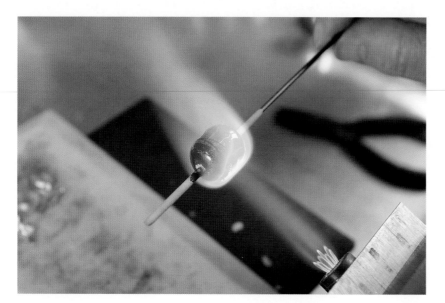

Heat the bead to a red glow. You will see the intense black stringer "bloom" a little. If it still looks like a solid line, heat it even more. Try to keep the high heat away from the ends of the bead to maintain nice even holes. Now work on getting the shape of the bead correct.

Heat and squash it.

Flip and press again. I am using Oneida ice tongs, but you can use any squashers.

You can easily see the chill marks here.

Flame polish them smooth. Check the shape and use the paddle to make any necessary corrections.

Put in the kiln for annealing.

After it has been annealed, remove it from the mandrel and dry, and then etch it in a liquid glass-etching solution. A liquid etching solution is easier to use on beads than a cream, and different brands may have different directions, so be sure to read them. Etching solutions are dangerous, so be careful and follow the directions. Be sure to wear eye protection, keep it off your skin, and store it in a clearly marked bottle in a safe place.

Place the bead (or beads) to be etched in a container; I like to use a Pyrex measuring cup because the etching solution isn't strong enough to affect it, and it is easy to pour back into the jar.

Carefully pour the solution into the container until the beads are covered. Let them etch for as long as the directions indicate, stirring very gently every few minutes so you don't get unetched spots where the beads are touching each other or the cup.

When time is up, carefully pour the solution back into the bottle and place the cup under running water.

When the water turns clear, I take the beads out and rinse them again, being sure to rinse the holes. Once the beads are dry, the etching will be evident. For only one bead, you can string it on fishing line, hang it in the bottle, and then remove and rinse it.

There are commercial resists available if you don't want the entire bead etched. A white glue also works well. Use a tiny brush or even a toothpick to paint it on the bead where you want the glass to remain shiny. Be sure to let it dry completely before etching, and then scrub it off.

101 More Inspirations

This list is just a beginning. Add more items as you think of them and keep it growing. As a challenge, choose a number at random from 1 to 101, look it up on the list, and use that as inspiration to make a bead.

1. Air
2. Earth
3. Water
4. Fire
5. All four elements (#1–4) in the same bead
6. Your zodiac sign
7. Clouds
8. Sunset
9. Mountains
10. Meadows
11. Rocks
12. Pebbles
13. Stones, such as turquoise, lapis, amethyst, and so on
14. Flower
15. Extreme close-up of a flower
16. Tree in different seasons
17. Tree bark
18. One of the four seasons or all on the same bead
19. NASA photos of outer space
20. A planet
21. Comet
22. Sun
23. Moon
24. Stars

A group of artifact beads made using baking soda.

25. A country (France, Morocco, Egypt, and so on)
26. Area of the United States (Southwest, Deep South, Florida, West Coast, New England)
27. Light
28. Music genre (jazz, heavy metal, punk, folk, polka, opera)
29. Your favorite song
30. An emotion (happiness, sadness, anger, boredom, hope, despair)
31. An opposite emotion
32. Fruit (tomato, peach, grapes, kiwi, banana)
33. Vegetable (pepper, onion, asparagus)
34. Candy (chocolate, hard candy, candy canes)
35. Bottles (look at shapes in particular)
36. Botanical shape (milk pod, thistle, acorn, seed)
37. Fabrics (go to a fabric store or look through your closet)
38. Rug (especially Persian rugs)
39. An animal
40. Your pet
41. Fantasy animal (dragon, unicorn)
42. Fantasy person (mermaid, wizard)
43. Piece of furniture
44. Fence
45. Gate
46. Bird (crow, hummingbird, robin, blue jay)
47. Butterfly
48. Moth
49. Insect
50. Door
51. Knots
52. Ladder
53. Middle of the night

Moons made with enamels and fine silver wire.

54. Noon
55. Time
56. One design element only, such as dots or lines
57. Paper clip
58. One color
59. Two colors and make ten different beads
60. A color and its opposite on the color wheel
61. Painting
62. Historical bead, such as warring states, melon, dZi, or eye bead
63. Favorite book
64. Children's book
65. Favorite movie
66. House
67. Cave
68. Grass
69. Weeds
70. Fish
71. Yourself
72. Totem pole
73. Seashell
74. Barnacles
75. Whale
76. Ship or boat
77. Anemone
78. Touch
79. Taste
80. Smell
81. Sound
82. Sight
83. Soft

A silver glass dot bead, highly reduced.

84. Hard
85. Flexible
86. Metamorphosis
87. Human eye
88. Lizard eye
89. Cat eye
90. Hand
91. Hair
92. Gears
93. Bicycle
94. Office building
95. Movement of a whale or dolphin
96. Vines
97. Tiles
98. Shoe
99. Man's tie
100. Dream or nightmare
101. Go for a walk with your digital camera and take a photo

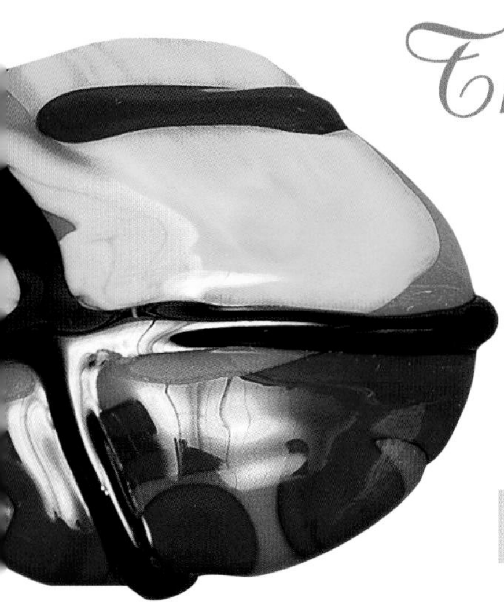

The Bead Makers

Louise Mehaffey

Laura Drosner Schreiber

Tamara Melcher

Katy Abbott

Patti Cahill

Alice St. Germain

Christel Hoffmann

Nolly Gelsinger

Louise Mehaffey

The Glass Place
eGlassplace.com

Laura Drosner Schreiber

Lampwork by Laura
lampworkbylaura.com

Over the years, I have taught art from the preschool level through adult education and have moved all around the country with my family. I experimented with many different media: pencil, clay, watercolor and oil painting, weaving, and more. In the early '70s, I decided to learn how to make a stained glass window to replace an ugly plastic one in my house, and glass became my obsession.

I created stained glass for many years, and in the process I explored sandblasting glass, painting and firing it, and fusing, and then in 1998, discovered lampworking. I love the immediacy of working on a torch, and I am transfixed by the colors and movement of the molten glass. Glass beads are my focus. They are an art form that can stand on its own or be combined with other beads to create jewelry. I love the thought that hundreds of years from now, someone will find one of my beads, feel the energy that created it, and wonder about the artist who made it.

My beads are inspired by nature in many ways. I love it when my beads are mistaken for natural stones. Also, the effortless lines in nature inspire me, as do the textures and colors. Always, the colors! Lately I have been decorating my beads with more and more dots; I am not sure where that is coming from, but I am willing to take the ride and see where it leads.

Before lampworking, I was a painting major at college, but I left that to be "in the real world." I worked in a restaurant and then at a home supply store, where I was the paint and home décor manager and kitchen designer. After a two-year office job, I became a full-time bead maker.

I tried just about all mediums, from bookmaking to wheel-thrown pottery, and then I found stained glass. I fell in love with glass, but I disliked the exactness of cutting and fitting the stained glass pieces. I found Cindy Jenkins's book *Making Glass Beads* at a local bookstore and thought melting glass looked like fun, so I bought a beginner kit and haven't looked back. I made my first beads in January 1998.

Many of my inspirations come from fabrics, especially modern prints from the '50s and '60s. I also like to explore the way light moves through glass, mixing transparent and opaque layers of color. I just like to play with color, color, and more color!

Tamara Melcher

The Clear Bead
theclearbead.com • tamaramelcher.com

I've had a full history of art-making before coming to glass. I went to art school in both Boston and San Francisco before landing in New York City. There I painted large abstract geometric acrylic paintings in the '60s. Next I had a period of fabric involvement, which included painting on silk, printing on cotton, appliqué, and collage that went into clothing. I had a shop in Soho, New York. Then came more painting, which became more and more dimensional. Love of color is the thread that ties it all together.

I discovered glass in 2000. It was the color and the motion of the hot glass that grabbed me and hasn't let go. A few years ago, I began to take macro photographs of my beads and print them, and that has taken me on another journey that feels more like painting. The pieces in the photographs have actually morphed into glass drawings, with no holes, but I will continue to make beads as well.

I am particularly inspired by nature, especially plant forms and the beautiful delicate color of flowers. In my photographic images of the glass, I have been inspired by meditation experiences that involve color and motion and a desire to see it more fully and share it with others.

Katy Abbott

Abbott Glass Designs
abbottglassdesigns.com

I was working on a graduate degree in gerontology when a friend showed me how to make necklaces out of beads. I fell in love. Every once in a while, I would come across a fantastic handmade glass bead and would be shocked by the price. What? Twenty dollars for one bead? Really? So I decided I needed to learn how to do it myself. And thousands of dollars later in equipment, supplies, classes, and Band-Aids, I am able to create just about anything I can dream up. I soon realized that making beads keeps me sane. For me, it is a form of meditation or prayer. I am forced to stay in the moment and am continually reminded to respect the flame and the glass. What started as a hobby has turned into the essence of who I am. My husband will frequently suggest that I go make beads when I am cranky. It is a therapy that always helps to center me.

In 1997, I started making beads on a Hot Head torch—and my husband ran out to buy me a fire extinguisher. Then in 1999, I purchased a used Minor Bench Burner by Nortel and have been delighted ever since.

What inspires me? The short answer is everything. Throughout the course of a day I can be in downtown Philadelphia admiring architecture and fashion or at the nature center a block from my house admiring the pattern on the back of a tortoise or the way a leaf falls from a tree. I am drawn into working with glass because it allows me to manipulate color, pattern, and shape.

Patti Cahill

Dyed in the Fire Designs
patticahill.etsy.com

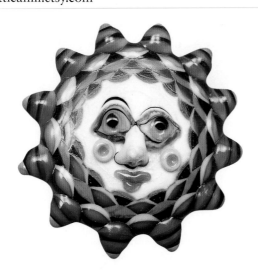

Before beads, I worked in commercial art, specializing in technical communication visuals, and then for a software development company that specialized in commercial art software. I was lead senior technical writer for one of the product teams.

In 1995, a one-day workshop on a Hot Head torch introduced me to glass beads, and I bought that torch so I could make beads at home. About a year later, when my company converted from a pension plan to a 401(k) plan, I got some "free" money and took a two-day workshop using a Nortel Minor Bench Burner. I bought all the upgraded equipment that weekend, and in 1998, I became a full-time glass bead maker.

I am inspired by color and pattern. I never look at other beads for inspiration. Rather, I try to pull in other aspects and interests in my life: eighteenth- and nineteenth-century botanical illustrations, things from nature such as plants and insects, aquatic life, fine art, folk and outsider art, fabric and tile patterns, and even clothes people wear to bead shows, to name just a few.

Alice St. Germain

Succulent Glass
succulentglass.com

Before I found glass, I was seriously perusing the metal arts. I also loved every kind of opal, tourmaline, and fantasy-cut quartz. My first step onto the beaded path, innocently enough, was learning how to knot pearls. Prior to that, beads hadn't made an impression. It wasn't long after that I discovered folks were making their own glass beads, choosing whatever gem-like color they wanted. It was an idea that hit me like a lightning bolt.

I took a beginning lampworking class in the fall of 1995 at a local arts center. Our torches were Hot Heads attached to MAPP gas canisters. The instructor was a fantastic cheerleader, encouraging us through our first attempts. About my third try, I made a wadge of unintended brown glass, and our teacher's response was to compliment me on trying color mixing. It was a great lesson, to see the potential in the actual results as opposed to seeing just a failed idea.

I don't think I can describe just one thing that inspires me. I find myself drinking in scenes of color: a handmade ceramic bowl full of amazing squash, a Japanese maple at peak color in the fall, a curious rock on the ground. From silk scarves to tropical plants, I am always making mental notes about color, texture, and shape.

Christel Hoffmann

Christel Productions Limited, Inc
christelsbeads@aol.com

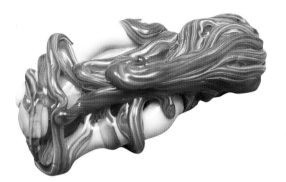

Nolly Gelsinger

Nollys Folly Studio
nollysfolly.com

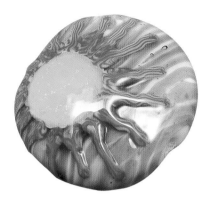

I graduated from Boston University in 1988 with a BFA in metals/jewelry and minors in art history and geology. I started my business, working mostly with sterling silver and semiprecious stones. In 1990, I took classes in glass blowing, which was my introduction to hot glass. I liked it, but prefer to work on a smaller scale.

That smaller scale was discovered in 1997, when I hosted Kristina Logan while she was teaching lampworking for the Pennsylvania Guild of Craftsmen, although I didn't take my first lampworking class until 1999. From then on, glass bead making was added to my repertoire of jewelry-making skills. I have taken many workshops in hot glass and metal, including the Precious Metal Clay Guild's certification class in 2002.

In general, my work is inspired by natural objects: marine and terrestrial flora and fauna and also foods and color, which has always been a major player in my jewelry. Before glass, the color came from metal patination, vitreous enameling, faceted gemstones, and natural stone beads. The glass palette is very large now, and sometimes it is a group of colors that spurs me on to a single bead or to an entire project where beads are just an element. Other times color inspiration comes from a client's color choices.

I have always been interested in crafty things. I tried knitting, crocheting, crewel embroidery, and various other things, but painting was the main thing for me. I have done many kinds of painting, most recently using a decorative style to embellish wooden boxes and wall hangings. The scrolls and flourishes on my beads come from both crewel work and decorative painting.

My first beadmaking class was during the summer of 2002, and that was the beginning of my glass obsession. I am fortunate to get time on the torch nearly every day, and my skills have been developed and honed with the mentoring of many beadmaking friends, both in local groups and online.

My inspirations are many. Traditional beads, many with Victorian scrolls, and organic metal reactions really interest me. My love of flowers has led to my sculptural glass flowers, and I enjoy creating new flowers in new colors. The invitation to participate in challenges for this book came as a welcome stimulus into new directions in beadmaking. It has been an eye-opening experience, both in having to explain why I chose to represent the challenges as I did, and in interpreting the idea into a glass bead.

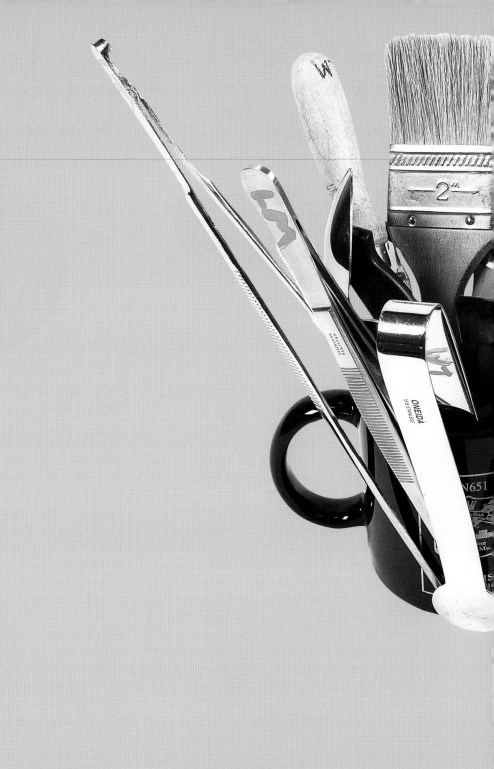

Supplies and Resources

Lampworking supplies and equipment

Arrow Springs
4301 A Product Drive
Shingle Springs, CA 95682
(800) 899-0689
arrowsprings.com

Frantz Art Glass & Supply
130 West Corporate Road
Shelton, WA 98584
(360) 426-6712 • (800) 839-6712
frantzartglass.com • frantznewsletter.com

Wale Apparatus
400 Front Street
P.O. Box D
Hellertown, PA 18055
(610) 838-7047 • (800) 334-9253
waleapparatus.com

Other Supplies

Containers & Packaging Supply, Inc.
1345 East State Street
Eagle, ID 83616
(208) 939-0291 • (800) 473-4144
containerandpackaging.com
Tins, bottles, and containers of all kinds

Lee Valley Tools
P.O. Box 1780
Ogdensburg, NY 13669-6780
(800) 267-8735
leevalley.com
Woodworking tools and supplies, including watch-maker cases

Rio Grande
7500 Bluewater Road N.W.
Albuquerque, NM 87121
(800) 545-6566
riogrande.com
Jewelry-making supplies and tools, including fine silver wire

Small Parts
P.O. Box 81226
Seattle, WA 98108-1226
(800) 220-4242
smallparts.com
Tubing, hardware, fasteners, and more, including steel tubes

Thompson Enamel
P.O. Box 310
Newport, KY 41072
(859) 291-3800
thompsonenamel.com
Enamels and enameling supplies

Resources

International Society of Glass Beadmakers (ISGB)
isgb.org
A nonprofit organization dedicated to promoting and supporting the art of making handcrafted, lampwork glass beads. There are many smaller bead societies throughout the United States, each with its own emphasis. An Internet search may find one near you.

Lampwork Etc
lampworketc.com
As its logo states, it's "a friendly place to bring together glass and jewelry artists."

Wet Canvas
wetcanvas.com
Artist's community with articles, news, and forums.

Bead Magazines

Check the Internet or your local bookstore for the bead magazines being published today. Many of them list bead societies, shops, and events.

Contributing Artists

Kevin Brett
Soul Imagery
soul-imagery.com
Fine art images and photography services

W. Eugene Burkhart Jr.
geneburkhart.com
International floral designer and pressed flower artist

Adrienne Trafford
adriennetrafford.blogspot.com
Artist and illustrator